There and Back

There and Back

by

Roy Porter

edited by
David Keller

Bayou Press

First published 1991 by
Bayou Press Ltd
117 High Street
Wheatley
Oxford
OX9 1UE

British Library Cataloguing in Publication Data

Porter, Roy 1923–
 There and back.
 1. Jazz. Biographies
 I. Title II. Keller, David
 785.42'092'4

ISBN 1–871478–30–8

Typeset by Opus, Oxford
Printed in the United States of America

Dedication

To my son Daryl Roy Porter, without whose words of encouragement this book would not exist, and to Daryl Nieanna Porter, my grand-daughter – all my love.

Contents

Acknowledgements

We should like to thank and acknowledge the assistance of the many individuals whose memories and good wishes contributed to this book.

The plate sections consist of photographs drawn from the author's collection, and are reproduced by permission. Grateful acknowledgement is made to the following for prints made available: Dan Audain, Wally Berman, Lucy Criss, Eric and Sadie Dolphy, Mason Dooley, Howard Moorehead, Phil Schaller and Kevin Stapleton. A special thank you also to James Graves and Carlos Quiroga for a job well done in the reproduction of old negatives and photographs.

The author is also indebted to Shirley Klett for all her efforts in compiling the discography.

Roy Porter
David Keller

Foreword

Roy Porter was the first and best bebop drummer resident in California. A few other names have been mentioned but Roy was it. He was the percussionist Charlie Parker hired for one of his finest sessions – *Moose the Mooche*, *Ornithology*, *Night in Tunisia*, *Yardbird Suite* – in March of 1946. Nobody else in LA was up to that sort of date then. Roy also figured in Bird's historic breakdown session that produced the moving and tragic version of *Lover Man*. Porter was the rhythmic stoker for such greats as Dexter Gordon and Teddy Edwards during those vibrantly creative years of the late 1940s. In addition he led one of the most interesting and underrated big bands of that entire period, featuring, among others, Art Farmer, Jimmy Knepper, Eric Dolphy, Teddy Edwards and Clifford Solomon. It is a scandal that this important orchestra's recorded output has been only partially reissued. Those tracks which have seen the light of day amply demonstrate that Roy could drive a large aggregation with tremendous propulsion. R. P. well understood the teachings of Kenny Clarke, Max Roach and Big Sid Catlett, but was no mere imitator of any of these gentlemen. His playing was infused with his own dash and verve, a positive swagger that lent authority to any rhythm section of which he was a part. Roy indelibly wrote some tasty pages of history in the Bebop Bible. Now he's written his life story, warts and all, and of one point you can be sure – it is nothing but the truth. Roy Porter is a man who has brought a deep down honesty to everything he has done. As one of the key survivors of the golden age of modern jazz, Roy is in an excellent position to set the record straight and illuminate some poorly

documented but significant areas of the music and the men
who made it.

Mark Gardner

Introduction

Roy Porter is a jazz drummer and composer whose place in the history of this great music is secured by his recordings with Charlie Parker during the Dial sessions of 1946. For this future generations will remember him. But, in addition Roy Porter is an example of a vanishing breed – the jazz survivor. Porter was there on the scene from the first set to the early-morning after-hours session. He is in a position to chronicle a fascinating portion of jazz history.

The archetypal bebop drummer has seen good times and those not so good, too. Along with the highs of performing with many of the legends of the jazz world such as Parker, Dexter Gordon, Howard McGhee and Sonny Criss, among others, Porter suffered also the lows of racism, discrimination, poverty, incarceration and drug addiction. The dark side of the music business was one he knew all too well from 1941 up until 1953, when he was finally arrested for narcotics possession on the streets of San Francisco. Yet whereas some became embittered, withdrawn or sullen about the glamorous *demi-monde* of jazz, Porter's story is one of hope.

Porter chronicles his life, warts and all, but then, rather than reveling in the role of outlaw hero, he moves along. He is not afraid to discuss that considerable portion of his life of all-night performances and the attendant hustling and con for the drug score which kept him going. Yet he does not glorify this period or the role junk played in his life. As part of a social phenomenon of virtually epidemic proportions (like it or not, the strung-out jazz musician was a reality), his narrative will perhaps help to lay to rest many of the glamorous clichés about the addict jazz musician. It is his ability to recognize his past for what it is that sets Porter apart from others.

For this and other reasons that become clear upon reading this man's story, Roy Porter's is a positive account. He has quite literally been there and now he is back. His story will perhaps provide some hope for today's youth as well as offering a fresh perspective on a much misunderstood portion of America's musical history. Additionally, it seeks to shed some light onto the heady days when bebop was a revolutionary development in music – both musically and socially – and to portray some of its lesser-known proponents. This book illuminates the importance of Los Angeles as a jazz center by examining the hot-house years of the 1940s, when jazz could be heard throughout the city, particularly up and down Central Avenue.

I first met Porter in 1980 when I interviewed a variety of Los Angeles musicians for a *Jazz Times* story on Eric Dolphy. Dolphy performed in Porter's big band and is remembered fondly by the bandleader as someone who was clearly on his way. During those first few meetings I detected a certain amount of scepticism in Porter and remembered his parting words. After I had interviewed him and was packing up, Porter said, "Next time you do a story, do it on someone who's still alive." His words stuck with me, and when the opportunity to interview him for *Coda* magazine came along I wrote his story. Over the course of those first meetings it became obvious to me that Porter had a fascinating tale to tell. After the initial article came out we stayed in contact, and when the possibility occurred I jumped at the chance to co-author Porter's book.

I have watched the development of Roy Porter during these years. He has changed, not in any obvious ways, but in subtler areas. Perhaps this is merely the result of two individuals getting to know one another, but it seems to be much deeper than this. Although Porter himself would downplay its significance, I have watched him change from a man with a chip on his shoulder, possessed of a rather cynical, world-weary attitude, to someone who knows both his contributions and his foibles. And while Porter is no longer actively playing these days, his story will surely provide enthusiasm for both future "drum beaters" and fans alike.

In times when the cult of self and holdovers from the "me decade" seem all too common, Porter's candor, appreciation, spirit and love for this music and those who were a part of that path-breaking movement known as bebop are a refreshing change.

David Keller

1

Bop City

New Year's Day 1951: we were playing for a receptive audience. The band was a quintet from the Blackhawk led by Vido Musso, the tenor saxophonist who had recorded the hit *Come Back to Sorrento* with Stan Kenton's big band. It also featured Vernon Alley on bass, Richard Wyands on piano and Pony Poindexter on alto saxophone. The audience was out of sight. We were really burning in this dining hall, where there must have been a thousand people. I looked out into that sea of faces and I saw people that knew all of us. They were hanging on to every note that we played.

That was 1951, but in that place a New Year's Day concert took place annually. So I returned in 1952. This time, however, I was with a band that included Sonny Criss, Dexter Gordon, Hampton Hawes and a bassist named Skippy Warren, and we were cooking again for that same beautiful audience. My drums seemed to be talking back to me. That crowd knew us and we knew a lot of them.

Just the same, I couldn't get down into that audience and talk with any of those familiar faces because I was on stage in the dining hall, right in the middle of San Quentin prison. Each year at the prison during those days the prisoners got a treat when musicians and entertainers came in and put on a show for them.

The most appreciative audience that I ever played for was made up of prisoners. I recognized a lot of my friends. People that I'd seen on the street, and people that I'd had dealings with – hustlers, pimps, dealers, heroin addicts. Musicians too, like Saunders King, the blues guitarist, who'd fallen on hard times since he'd had his nationwide hit *S. K.*

Blues a few years earlier. I looked out in the audience and saw all these people that I knew from the streets.

This memory is vivid because I had just played for the inmates on New Year's in 1951 and 1952. Then, in June of 1953, I came through those same gates, those big green walls, those catwalks with the armed guards on them. I'd just been busted for being a junkie, and when I came through the gates this guard who was processing all of us says, "Yeah, motherfucker, we knew you was gonna be comin' through here again. We knew you was high. That's why you was playin' so good last New Year's. We knew we'd see you soon, Roy."

The feeling of entering a prison is indescribable. It is tough, especially if you are used to your freedom. That was one of the things that was part of my life in San Francisco during that period. I was an addict. It was a dark cloud over my life there. After a few weeks the shock finally wore off. I lay awake nights pondering the reasons for my ending up a convict in the penitentiary.

I came to San Francisco originally in 1946 as a member of Howard McGhee's sextet. But that was just for a six-week stint at the Backstage Club on Powell Street. A little later, in 1950, I came back to San Francisco with Sonny Criss for a job at the Wolf Club in Oakland. Somehow I just stayed on. I didn't know how long I was going to stay there. I really was just making the gig with Sonny Criss because it was pretty good money. I'd just finished recovering from an automobile accident which had occurred while I was out on the road in New Mexico with my big band and was in rough financial shape. So I decided to take the job. Along with Sonny and me there were Hampton Hawes on piano and Joe Stone on bass. That was about the first occasion when any name jazz artists had ever really played in Oakland.

Oakland at that time was a city that did not have a lot of nightclubs. The ones that were there were mostly country-and-western, swing and rhythm-and-blues places that were in the black neighborhoods. One of the most well-known black nightclubs was Slim Jenkins' Supper Club. It was an attractive, large club that booked name artists, mostly blues musicians, with a floor show and dancing. It was located on East 14th Street on the main drag in Oakland.

The Wolf Club was a swinging place. It was the first club in the area to hire jazz musicians. It was a bit off the beaten path, but we drew clientele that wanted to hear the new music of that time. The people that came were basically enthusiasts, and since the club had a no-dancing policy serious fans did come out. Black people, white people, Orientals, Hispanics, beatniks – they all really came out to hear you. They'd come from Berkeley and the small cities surrounding the Bay Area, as well as from San Francisco over the Bay Bridge, that monstrously beautiful piece of architecture. At that time you could also make the trip by ferry.

The Wolf Club's hours of business were from 9.30 p.m. to 1.30 a.m., and everybody positively had to be out of there by 2.00 a.m. The music played was bebop jazz, similar to what was being played in San Francisco at Bop City. In my experience you can play any kind of music that you want when a club has a no-dancing policy. This is so much more exciting, since you are more or less totally free to express yourself.

The first time I met Ray Charles was at the Wolf Club in 1950. He was playing somewhere in Berkeley or Oakland and came by to hear us on his off night. After the gig we went back to his hotel and shot up smack together. Ray had a small group called the Ray-o-Vacs, had made a number of hit records, and was well on his way.

The gig at the Wolf Club was great but it didn't last more than four weeks. Still, I saw a lot of people there, like Damita Jo, the singer who had been with my big band and who had just joined Steve Gibson and his Red Caps group. In fact, she later married Steve. There we got a chance to play songs like *Cherokee, Night in Tunisia, Ornithology, Willow Weep for Me* and many of the tunes that would later become jazz standards. It was such a relaxed, mellow atmosphere you could stretch out and blow chorus after chorus of those tunes.

At about this time a man named Jimbo Edwards offered us a job at Bop City, a little after-hours place he operated in San Francisco. Sonny Criss, Hampton Hawes, Joe Stone and I were the first musicians of any note that were hired at his club. In a real sense, we were the musicians that helped put Bop City on the map.

During that period I got to know more about Hampton Hawes. Hamp was the son of a minister and grew up in Los Angeles. But Hamp was a person who quickly found out that a musician's life and life on the streets was a far cry from the teachings of his father. When I knew him earlier on, Hampton was rather shy and was an introvert both on and off the stand. He was very shy around women and just about all situations which demanded an outgoing personality – that is, until he became strung out. Hampton was not a schooled pianist, being instead largely self-taught, particularly when it came to jazz. But to me he was one of the greatest piano players of all time.

We met these two chicks one night at the Wolf Club. Penny was a redhead and Dottie a blond. They were best friends and were together most of the time. Penny had eyes for me and Dottie for Hamp. Penny knew I was using, but Dottie didn't know Hamp was. Later on, when both Hamp and I were gigging at Bop City, Dottie found out that Hamp was using. When this got back to Hamp, he was devastated. I told him to forget it and said, "If Dottie digs you, it makes no difference what you are." Nonetheless, Hamp and Dottie remained tight for many years. Penny and I remained friends until her death in 1979. Shortly after our gig at Bop City in 1951, Hamp moved back down to Los Angeles and our paths didn't cross again for many years.

When we started working there, Bop City began attracting a serious jazz audience. And Jimbo wasn't even charging admission then. Jimbo was a smart man. Even though he couldn't read or write his name, he was quite keen upstairs. So when people dropped by regularly to attend his club with its after-hours policy, he began charging admission. All sets were 45 minutes on the stand and 15 off. Bop City really started taking off when Jimbo instituted a jam sessions policy. As business began picking up and the club started to get a name, we were paid a little more.

Unlike Oakland, San Francisco was a jumping city. Bop City was a small club that was located on the corner of Post and Buchanan streets in San Francisco. If you blinked an eye you missed it. When we opened the club, the bandstand was quite small in the back of the room. There was a little coffee shop in front which served breakfast. The waitresses worked both the coffee shop and the back room where we were playing. After Jimbo remodeled it, it seated maybe 100 people maximum. He knocked out the back part of the room, enlarging it, and moved the bandstand over to the side. When the club got famous a large sign went up and people would line up outside to get in.

Bop City was located in the Fillmore District, which was predominantly black. There were many clubs on Fillmore, Sutter, Post, Bush, Buchanan and Geary. Most of the other places were before-hours spots like the Champagne Supper Club on Post and Fillmore, which had dancing and a floor show. Across the street was the Alabam Club, which also had a dancing policy. The Black and Tan Bar & Grill had a strong music policy also. There were really so many great rooms there, since the Fillmore District was the hub of what was happening in those days.

Because Bop City was an after-hours club you brought your own liquor and bought set-ups. No liquor was supposed to be sold after 2.00 a.m., but that policy didn't seem to be taken all that seriously. People of all descriptions – black, white, rich, poor, famous, beautiful women, stars, bums, beatniks, addicts, pimps, hustlers, whores, nuns, priests – just about the whole gamut were there to dig what the musicians were playing. And many great musicians sat in too. Greats like Mr B., Billy Eckstine, sang there until we closed at 6.00 a.m. one morning, just because he dug the atmosphere and music. He was appearing at the Fairmont Hotel on Nob Hill and came by after his gig ended.

As a member of the house rhythm section at Bop City I had

a ball. And the job for me was really not that strenuous. It seemed like all of the musicians that were appearing locally would come by to join at that club, people like Dizzy Gillespie, Miles Davis, Illinois Jacquet, Lionel Hampton, Buddy Rich, Art Blakey and most all of the strong jazz players. After musicians finished playing at the Blackhawk or wherever they were at 1.30 a.m., they could always make the Bop City gig at 2.00 a.m. This was a nice arrangement for me and I made this six times a week, if I wasn't sick from my habit, since the club was dark one night a week. Bop City took off like a rocket. I suppose it was a case of being in the right place at the right time. Seemed like every musician that came to San Francisco would fall by Bop City. That was one of the main reasons I stayed on in San Francisco.

The food was acceptable at Bop City, but it was a distant second to the music which, of course, was the primary attraction. Right around the corner on Buchanan Street was Jackson's Nook. It was a 24-hour restaurant and was a nice clean place run by a Mr Jackson and his wife. If you wanted quality food that was really the place to go. Once Ray Nance, Duke Ellington's marvelous trumpet player and great violinist, and I had breakfast at Jackson's Nook, just before Ray passed. He too had a narcotics problem.

In Frisco I played with some of the greatest, but Mr Sonny Criss, the great alto saxophonist, was my personal favorite. He had more soul in his little finger than the average dude has in his whole body. Sonny Criss is one of the few people whom I've known that I completely loved. He was just too much. I've seen Sonny cry, I've seen him go through a lot of changes behind alcohol, drugs and family problems, but when Sonny was up on the bandstand there were few who could touch him. The world never got to know the real Sonny Criss. But if you'll listen to his recording of *Willow Weep for Me* you'll know what I'm talking about. And as far as being a complete human being, not just an extremely talented musician, Sonny was tops. He was deep inside.

From my observations most people are shallow. I hope this doesn't offend any of the other musicians that I've played with, those who are supposed to be my friends and all. Sonny was not plastic like 95 per cent of people are. You really had to know the man, really know him, not just hear him play or listen to his albums. I mean really know the individual. And I didn't even see Sonny all that much towards the end, but I always knew where I stood with him. The world lost one of the greatest talents in music when Sonny died, and it still hasn't recognized his importance yet. That's a tragedy.

During this same time period, shortly after the Wolf Club closed down, I began working before hours at one of the more famous jazz joints in San Francisco, the Blackhawk. It was located on the corner of Turk and Hyde streets in the Tenderloin District. The Tenderloin was filled with flop houses, winos, drug users and other characters and was in an ethnically mixed area.

Johnny and Helen Noga ran the club when I was there. They were people who had class and who had really built up a good clientele. They did not feature a strictly jazz policy, mixing it up with a lot of blues and popular acts as well. Yet most of the greats of the jazz world did play there, including Miles Davis, Gerry Mulligan, Erroll Garner, Johnny Hodges, Dizzy Gillespie, Benny Carter, the Red Norvo Trio with Charles Mingus, Oscar Peterson, Sarah Vaughan, Art Pepper, Art Tatum and Lester Young, among so many others.

Vernon Alley, the bassist whom I call Mr San Francisco, worked the club more than anyone locally. I think a great deal of Vernon because he was the first musician who gave me a regular before-hours job at the Blackhawk after I decided to stay in San Francisco. Vernon organized a group composed of Richard Wyands on piano, Pony Poindexter on alto saxophone, himself on bass and myself on drums, and it became the house rhythm section at the Blackhawk. From then on out I had a steady gig there plus a steady after-hours job at Bop City.

At the Blackhawk we played jazz and commercial music. Pony Poindexter and Vernon would sing the Jon Hendricks type of things in harmony and would put on a little show.

We also played the popular jazz tunes of the day and backed a lot of top-notch vocalists such as Ernie Andrews, Sarah Vaughan, Dinah Washington and Anita O'Day, among others. We worked with Vido Musso, the Italian boy who played with Stan Kenton. He came to San Francisco from Los Angeles and picked up his rhythm section at the club. I also worked with Benny Carter in the same type of situation. That band included Gerald Wiggins and Charlie Drayton.

One week Vernon's group played opposite Dave Brubeck at the Blackhawk. That was the first time I had heard of Brubeck. He was on piano with Ron Crotty on bass and Cal Tjader on drums. Brubeck was just trying to get his thing together at that time and to me he wasn't really sounding all that cool . . . I'll leave it at that.

Alley's band didn't just play the Blackhawk. One night we played a show downtown at a club backing the great Josephine Baker. A most embarrassing incident happened that night. Josephine Baker snagged the bottom of one of her fabulous gowns on the stage screw that was in front of my bass drum. I got all flustered, but she quickly told me, "Don't worry young man. It's not your fault. Besides, I have plenty of gowns." That made me feel a lot better. And Josephine Baker was quite a presence.

During this same time Chico Hamilton came through with Lena Horne. After joining Lena he finally got his sound together on drums. Then Lena and her group were playing the Fairmont Hotel. Whenever Chico came to San Francisco he'd look me up and we'd get together.

The last time I saw my main man, one of the all-time greats, Mr Shadow Wilson, was in San Francisco. He came through there and played the Blackhawk with Erroll Garner. Erroll still had John Simmons on bass and was using Shadow on drums. I hate to say this, but Shadow and I did shoot up together because he was on the stuff by that time. And it wasn't too long after he left town that Shadow Wilson, the great drummer who was such an inspiration to me, was dead.

Another club in the Tenderloin which we used to frequent was the Say When on Bush Street. I remember seeing Harry "the Hipster" Gibson over there. Gibson was a white dude who played boogie-woogie piano and sang that jivey scat stuff. The man who ran the Say When was a racist called Dutch. He'd hire you but make it clear what he thought of Blacks. Billie Holiday worked for Dutch once during that time. He treated her like she was a dog, but since Billie was pretty strung out at that point, even her husband treated her that way, which didn't make it right. Still, if you take heroin that means that somebody else is controlling you.

One of the highlights, though, from that period was catching Art Blakey. Art Blakey had a band he was touring with, and after he finished his gig he came by and sat in at Bop City. But when Art got through playing, man you could forget it! And on my drums! When he finished it was my turn. He told me, "Hey look, get over on that big cymbal. Get off that high-hat cymbal. They ain't doing that no more, baby!"

Another bad dude that came through Bop City when I was working there was Buddy Rich. Yeah, Buddy Rich with his cocky ass, bad with his paradiddles and his technicalities. But for my money, he isn't a true modern-jazz drummer. But I respect Buddy Rich, you have to. Then we got to talking and what he was saying made a lot of sense. During the course of our conversation the subject came up about lessons and studying. I told him, "Man, I've never studied drums. I never had a practice pad." He replied, "I thought I was the only motherfucker that could say that. I've never had a practice pad either. When we get up on that bandstand we ain't playing no practice pads, are we? If I practice, I practice on my drums. I never owned a practice pad, no way!"

There were a lot of beautiful people in San Francisco then. Another drummer there was named Bernard Peters. With him you were really talking about technical ability. Bernie could get up on those drums, and while he wasn't that great playing with others, he could get up on the stand all by himself and play every technical thing that you'd ever want to hear. He was just about the baddest dude you'd ever want to hear technique-wise.

One of the bigger surprises of my life came one night when Frank Foster got on the stand. Now I didn't know this guy from Adam. He comes in with his horn, he's in a soldier suit and nobody was paying him too much attention. So he comes up and asks if he can play with us. This was just before our intermission break. The band that night was Leo Amadee on piano, Larry Lewis on bass, myself on drums and Teddy Edwards and Dexter Gordon on tenors (Sonny Criss had left by this time). So Frank got his horn out and he really wants to play. By and by he asks us, "Will you guys play with me?" And I thought, "Who is this dude? Who does he think he is?" Teddy and Dexter just got up and walked away. This didn't phase Frank Foster, who came up on the stage with us and started to play. When he got through playing, you could forget it. He was really blowing! And the situation was complicated further, since you're never supposed to snub anybody. The rhythm section stuck around more out of curiosity than anything, but when Frank Foster got through you should have seen the look on everyone's faces! He later joined Basie, playing and arranging. The solos he played on Basie's *Everyday* and *The Comeback* with Joe Williams are classics.

It's funny how life works. I have to mention another tenor player, a man who was already in 1950 off in the direction that Coltrane was to make popular. His name was Oyama Johnson and he had a truly original sound on tenor saxophone. Johnson was doing some music that was simply amazing. But I don't think many people ever heard much about him. Last time I saw Oyama Johnson he had come to San Quentin. Oyama got off into heroin. I remember seeing him in the joint there just before they transferred me to Chino.

One morning Dizzy Gillespie came by and sat in with us. Leo Amadee was sounding pretty nice that night on the piano, which was really only a raggedy upright with the front removed. Still, they did keep it in tune, since there were always greats dropping in to play. But as far as Dizzy's reputation goes, for sheer enthusiasm, there is really no one that can touch Diz. That night most everything clicked and we made a great deal of strong music.

After that swinging morning session I gave Diz a lift back home. I always had an automobile and at that point I owned a nice 1950 gray Oldsmobile 98. On the way home we stopped off and had breakfast together. Then after breakfast, when I was driving him down to his hotel, he began telling me, "Say, I'm sorry that you had your accident when you were out on the road with your big band. And I'm glad that nobody was seriously injured. But in a way I'm glad too that you did have that accident, because your band was bad, man!" And then he laughed that infectious laugh of his.

I have to say a bit more about Larry Lewis the bassist. Larry was one of my best friends up there. I loved him. He helped me kick a habit once and I'll never forget that. Larry was always trying to get me to stop using. So, one of the times I tried to quit, Larry stayed with me for a week and would tie me in the bed to keep me from getting up to go out and cop. Larry Lewis was a true friend, period. He wasn't what you would call great on bass, but he could certainly play well. But more importantly, as a person, he was a giant.

Another talented musician is Jerome Richardson. Most people know of Jerome Richardson, the great reeds man. But I remember Jerome when he was listening to Teddy Edwards and Dexter Gordon, trying to find his identity on his own horn. Now when Jerome was leading his band he would frequently call me up and say, "Man, we've got a gig. Can you make it? All I want you to do is just stay clean for this gig. Will you do that?" And I'd do it. That took a lot of guts, since in those days if you were a hype you wouldn't be getting hired by too many bandleaders. The stigma of being an addict was impossible to hide from your fellow musicians, as they all knew the score. But Jerome would at least call me for a gig.

Chuck Thompson, the drummer, was a hell of a musician

that came up from Los Angeles to San Francisco about the same time as I did. Chuck is the drummer who's featured on the recording called *The Chase* with Dexter Gordon and Wardell Gray. When I got busted Chuck was still in San Francisco too. Then eventually he had to go through the same things that I did. Eventually everybody that messed with heroin had to pay their dues.

But I've always felt that San Francisco was from another era and place. To me even the people were different. It's difficult to pin down, but the people seem to dress and act differently. I suppose that's partially because it's a night town, a night-life city. I know there's another side to it, a cultured one, but I never did get a chance to see much of that.

I did have some nice nights out on the town with Teddy Edwards. Teddy came up to San Francisco a bit later. I call him Johnny Come Lately to that Bop City scene, since he stepped in and filled the place that Dexter left when he split. Anyway, Teddy and I went downtown on a few occasions. Once I recall seeing the Harlem Globetrotters with him. This was the first time they'd played downtown. So we went down to the game together and had a pleasant evening. We also went downtown together to see Kid Gavilan, the welterweight champion. Gavilan was a black Cuban fighter who was famous for his bolo punch. He'd invented a loping, wind-up style punch that most of the people he fought couldn't get past.

San Francisco for me was a rollercoaster. There were some fantastic times when I was playing my ass off on the stand with Sonny Criss or Dexter Gordon. But then there were some dark days too. There was many a time when I would tie myself up with a necktie and put that needle in my arm by myself and, after I'd get through, sometimes I'd be down on my knees praying for the power to deliver me from that evil. But I couldn't help myself. I was struggling, but there were many, many times I'd be on my knees praying for the power to get out of that shit.

It was a mother to be a drug addict and shoot heroin. Any

person who puts a needle in his arm is a damn fool. I really never saw a chemically-free day for the three years that I was up in San Francisco. That's a fact that I'm not too proud of but that was the reality.

I can say, though, that I never ripped anybody off to pay for my habit. I had somewhere between a 50 and 75 dollar a day "Jones," which in the 1950s was quite a bit of money. I was always able to cover the cost of my habit, since I was working two jobs almost from the beginning. In addition, I always had a number of women around who treated me well and helped look after me – until they became tired of this habit and what it did to my personality.

I met a fox named Mary Lincoln in 1946 while in San Francisco, when I was with Howard McGhee's band at the Backstage Club. This chick was so fine that I snatched her. During that time I also had two more women in LA that were making big bread for me hustling. Blackie was foxy Chicano girl that worked the streets, and Virginia was a freckle-faced redhead white girl, built like a brick shithouse, who worked in a "house" in Hollywood. I had Virginia and Blackie come to San Francisco to meet Mary. We all had a pow-wow and it was agreed that Mary would join the Porter "family."

When I left San Francisco that first time in 1946, I brought Mary to Los Angeles and we all lived together until it got sticky. Mary said, "You don't need those bitches. I can make more money than both of them put together." And she proceeded to do just that and became my *main* squeeze. I kept Mary Porter (also known as Judy) until I went into the joint in 1953. But the most ironic part of the whole thing was that she had me fooled for three years. I had no idea that she was only 14 years old when I first met her.

But I always had a *good* woman to help me out, because Judy and I had been together off and on since 1946. But she eventually got tired of helping to support my habit, helping me kick so often, and then it wasn't doing any good. So she split – rightly so.

We lived all over the Fillmore District, on Bush Street, O'Farrel Street, Geary, Divisadero, Farren, among others, always in apartments. As long as I had my stuff everything was fine. At least you think everything is fine. You think that you are functioning, but you are just not. Heroin makes you feel as if everything in life is always fine as long as you have your "medicine."

In terms of my chemical dependence I had smoked pot since I was in junior high school, and had been drinking wine and dropping pills for years. The first time that I tried heroin, though, was in 1949 in Los Angeles, but I had shot some morphine and sniffed cocaine in 1948 in Cleveland, Ohio, when I was with Tiny Grimes. Anyway, that first time Von Streeter, a saxophone player with Johnny Otis's band, and I sniffed some "H." By the time I got to San Francisco, I had a Nose Jones or stomach habit. I kicked that a couple of times until I started shooting the shit.

I eventually did kick for good, but it was not the kind of help that I was expecting. They sent my ass to the penitentiary. That's the way it happened and in a way that was for the best. It takes a couple of years to get that poison out of your system and takes many more years to get it out of your mind. So I was very fortunate. I was on my knees asking for some kind of help and a higher power saw fit to give me some.

My long journey out of the darkness started routinely enough. I was working downtown in the International Settlement before hours with Stanley Morgan, the guitarist, who had a little group down there. Anyway, we were down there playing in this little establishment that was for strippers. The night I got busted Billie Holiday happened to be performing in town, down at the Say When club on Bush Street. Carl Drinkard, her piano player, came down to where we were working, since he had the day off. After I finished playing we went together to cop down on Geary Street, since Carl was using too.

The police in that district used to patrol the area on foot. For the most part the cops in and around that entire district didn't like black people in any shape, way or form. Since they had seen me around Bop City they got to know who I was, and they probably had a pretty good idea that I was using. This was really a pretty safe guess, since there were only a select few like Teddy Edwards that weren't.

That particular night I got out of the car and I told Carl, "Look, I'm going into this gambling joint. Just keep driving around the block. I'll make the connection." I went inside this pool hall and bought two papers, which was about 30 dollars' worth of heroin. Then I should have done what I usually did. Normally, I'd wrap the stuff up in cellophane and put it in my mouth. But that night I was so sick, and needed to get straight so bad, that I just put the papers in my pocket and walked out onto Geary. I got about ten feet from the corner. Bang, here's these two big Irish cops that turned the corner and were facing me. I walked towards them and got around them. When I was about three feet past them they turned around and said, "Hey," because they didn't recognize me at first. It was probably about two in the morning and I was trying to get to my after-hours job at Bop City. When they said that I went, "Oh, Goddamn. This is it." And I threw my stuff down, aiming for the gutter. Soon as that shit hit the gutter they had their flashlight on it. Then one of the motherfuckers said, "Okay, now run you black junkie son-of-a-bitch, so I can blow your nigger brains out. Run! Go on, try it!" And that was it for me. Luckily for Carl he kept right on driving.

Ironically this was probably the beginning of my life getting together as far as my heroin addiction was concerned. It was positive. Only six months before I had committed myself to the Napa State Hospital, unaware that it was a mental hospital, an institution that didn't really have the proper facilities for treating drug addicts. They knew the difference between a drug addict and someone who was mentally ill, but you were on the same ward with some of the less violent people that had mental problems. There I saw things that would make the average person nauseous. I saw mental patients receive electro-shock treatments that almost killed them, saw people stripped and placed into bath tubs filled with ice. After about two weeks of this I knew I had made a big mistake being there.

I stayed in the Napa State Hospital for 90 days. When my

time was up and I got out, the very day I was released and got home to San Francisco I saw the man and got me some stuff and was gone again. I wanted help, but I just wasn't strong enough. So the night I got popped I had been home for six months after having voluntarily committed myself. Heroin is truly a bad motherfucker. There ain't nothing badder than heroin but God and death, because the feeling that you get from it is so great that you can't even explain it. And the only thing that can make a heroin user violent is if he can't get his junk and he becomes sick and must have some more stuff. For the most part, as long as he's got his shit, he takes care of business. Some people will nod and scratch, others won't. There's different make-up in different people. I'd nod and scratch sometimes, and other times I wouldn't. I could go about my daily business.

The newer generation of addicts know nothing about what it was like to be a user in those days. In the first place you couldn't buy a syringe legally unless you were a diabetic and had a prescription for insulin. I had to buy an eyedropper and have a connection at a drug store to get a number 12 needle. I'd mix heroin and water in a spoon, heat it until it dissolved, put a piece of cotton in it, which was used to absorb the impurities, attach the dropper to the needle, draw it up into the dropper, tie myself up with a necktie and put that poison into my veins. That's the reason you were called a dirty hype.

As long as heroin addicts were confined mainly to black neighborhoods there was no "drug problem." It didn't even get too much notoriety. That didn't happen until it got to certain proportions with white kids in middle-class neighborhoods. When that happened all kinds of programs for rehabilitation sprang up. When we were using, if we were caught we went directly to jail, period.

They took my ass downtown to the City Jail when I was arrested. I stayed there for three months on a vagrancy addict charge. In addition, I did another ten days for having a switch-blade knife in my pocket. "Vag addict" was a law that held that if you had fresh needle marks or "tracks" on the veins in your arm, you could automatically get 90 days in jail because you were a heroin user.

I didn't make bail because I was working for a popcorn pimp by the name of Jimbo Edwards (who owned Bop City), who wouldn't even go my bail. And I was working for the dude! Now I understand why a lot of people who were supposed to be my friends didn't come down to the jail to see me. I suppose they figured that by coming down to see a junkie who was locked up they'd be labeled junkies. The police could also search all visitors – tell you to roll up your sleeves, strip search, you name it. And if you were a musician you were particularly suspicious in the mind of the police. In those days they could do anything to you, especially if you were black. A few people who couldn't help me did come by.

Being arrested at that time as a dope user was heavy. Technically you were held on a violation of the Health and Safety code – a felony. As such you had to have people with property for collateral to post your bail. Judy had no property but did come by to see me. But she was tired of my using and split. I didn't even blame her. Stanley Morgan came by to visit and a few select others. But they couldn't help. Yet, if I had been released on bail I would have started using right away again. So, everything probably happened for the best. Jimbo Edwards, however, was the only one in my crowd who owned property.

My bail wasn't even that high, $500 on a $2500 bond. That was all that had to be put up. But no, the person that I was working for wouldn't even go my bail. So I laid up there and kicked and saw junkies die next to me on nothing but iron cots in City Jail.

During my stay in City Jail I had my first migraine headache. But then I had no idea what it was. The night that I was taken into custody I had my reading glasses on me, but they always take all of your property when you are jailed and so somehow my glasses were lost, so they said. Bullshit. Anyway, I didn't have them any more all the while I was in City or County Jail. One night in my cell it felt as though a gun had exploded in my head above my eyes. I thought at that time it was because I didn't have my glasses. When I got to San Quentin they gave me glasses, but this didn't solve the problem and I continued to get these heavy, recurring headaches. It wasn't until I was out on the streets again in 1956 that these headaches were diagnosed as migraine. Migraine headaches are monstrous. I have had them so bad that I have put a 38 revolver to my head but didn't have the nerve to pull the trigger.

Finally, I was arraigned to San Bruno, south of San Francisco, where County Jail is located. There it was a little bit better. I was able to bathe and it was a bit more humane. But it was still jail, still really something else. My trial came up in June of 1953. The judge that sent me up was named Michelson. He was cold and hated drug addicts and black people, so I had two strikes against me going in there. All of the junkies, black or white, that went up before Judge Michelson got some time. When he sentenced me, he looked at me and said, "I'm going to do you a favor. I know who you are and I know that you have been able to earn a good living as a musician. But you are going to hate this decision. I'm going to do you a favor young man – nothing to six." That meant that I could do nothing or I could do six years. The way it worked out I did four years – two years in prison and two years out on parole.

The next thing I knew I was on my way to the joint and crying like a baby. Locked up: no overnight, like for some traffic ticket. Hell, I'd never even been in jail for *anything* before. But as much as I hate to say it, Judge Michelson did me a favor. I hated that motherfucker for two, maybe three years until it finally came to me. Today I don't think too kindly of him, but I do realize that he did me one of the biggest favors of my life, because otherwise I could have been dead.

When I got into prison there at San Quentin I was clean and feeling good because I had kicked in the City and County Jails. All I had to do in Quentin was "do my time." At San Quentin I'd go to the recreation area where there were basically remedial classes, and teachers for those who wanted to acquire an education. I went to the band room. There weren't actually that many musicians there that could really play, but they did have a band there. I was interested in the piano. Since I'd always messed with the piano I decided to get to know it better. In prison I first sat down at the piano and hit B flat, E flat, F, dah, dah, dah dah dah – then F sharp, down to F, E flat, C – dah, dah, dah, dah – B flat, dah, dah, E flat, back to C – and that was the beginning of *Lonesome Mood*.

Truthfully, I was sent to San Quentin, but because I didn't have a record I was not a prisoner in the big yard. That was where the people that were doing hard time were confined. I was in another section – the guidance center.

The guidance center is where every prisoner is kept for 90 days to determine where they will be confined to do their time. This all depends on whether you have previous arrests for crime or are a hardened criminal. This is called processing. If you are a habitual, hardened criminal you are sent to Folsom Prison. If you have been in trouble with felonies before you are kept there in San Quentin in the section called the "Big Yard." If you had no previous arrests you were sent to Chino Institute for Men in Southern California. Chino is a minimum security prison. You are there on your honor and can walk away if you want to. But, of course, if you do escape and are then caught you then go directly to either San Quentin, Soledad or even Folsom. So it all depends on you.

Prison was no picnic. I saw zip-gun shootings, rapes, fights, and a man fall out of line on the way to the mess hall dead with a shiv in his back. I got a break and, instead of being sent to San Quentin's Big Yard, Soledad or Folsom, I was sent to the Chino Institute for Men near Los Angeles because I didn't have a record.

These thoughts make me reflect on how my life began. My life has been a rich one – rich in experiences and memories.

2

Childhood

I was born in a little coal-mining camp called Lester in the mountains of Colorado on 30 July 1923. My mother was Charlotte Porter and my father was William Nelson Porter, a coal miner. I remember the little red wagon he brought home for me; the coal miner's lamp on his work cap and the strong image he left as my father, the greatest man in the world and the provider for his family – my mom, my sister Evelyn, who is four years my junior, and me. My parents were very religious. In his spare time on weekends my father would sell religious material such as books, magazines, bibles, etc. He did not smoke, drink or swear, something I sure did not inherit, I am sorry to say.

My father was from Knoxville, Tennessee. Whether he was born there I have no idea, as Mom never discussed it and I didn't push the issue. Dad was a mixture of black, Mongolian and English, and I do know he was not a subservient man. I presume I inherited that trait at an early age because no one has ever controlled me and never will. My mother was born Charlotte Chappell in Marshall, Texas. Her people were from Rule, Texas. I remember Johnny and Princella, her nephew and niece, coming to Colorado Springs during the summer. In fact mother gave Johnny our old Willys Knight car because she couldn't drive. I have lost track of these people. Maybe someday we will catch up to each other.

In coal mining you moved from camp to camp; when a mine would dry up you go to the next one. In 1928 we moved from Lester to a camp near Trinidad, Colorado, which is not too far from Walsenburg, Colorado, the county seat. On my birth certificate my place of birth is listed as

Walsenburg because Lester wasn't even on a map and became a ghost town. After a few months in Trinidad we got in our 1928 Willys Knight Phaeton four-door convertible and moved to Raton, New Mexico. I never will forget, as we left Trinidad, the white miners and families were taunting, "Bye Bye Blackbirds." To this day I can't stand that tune and never played it even as a request with my bands. At the time I couldn't understand why they were laughing and saying that.

My father didn't live long enough to really enlighten me about these things. In 1931, when I was only eight, William Porter caught pneumonia in the mines and died. He was only 54.

I was not aware that my father had left his family a home bought and paid for in full in Colorado Springs, Colorado. Colorado Springs was a beautiful little town of about 30,000 population at that time. It is situated at the foot of one of the famous mountains in the world, Pikes Peak. It was and still is considered a resort town for people of means, especially during the summer season. The famous Garden of the Gods and Cave of the Wind are situated near the foot of Pike's Peak. So is Manitou Springs, a suburban community of Colorado Springs, with its wells of spring water gushing from the ground. This water is supposed to have medicinal properties for people with arthritis, etc. It is a beautiful environment. People world-wide came to Colorado Springs for health and vacations.

The famous Pikes Peak Hill Climb Auto Races were held annually on Labor Day. Many of the famous auto racers like the Unsers would compete to reach the top and the finish line. It is very exciting and dangerous. The Peak is over 14,000 feet high and snow is at the top all year round.

When I was 13 years old I tried to hike up to the Peak with Jess Tarrant, our next-door neighbor. He was an adult and would hike up there each year to see the finish of the races. When we got about a mile from the top and could see the cars and the finish line, I was taken ill because the altitude was too high for me. We had to go back down, which was a very big disappointment for me. I always planned to try again – you've heard the expression "Pikes Peak or Bust" – but I never did.

The center of Colorado Springs was in between two railroad lines, the Denver and Rio Grande on the east side and the Santa Fe on the west side. We lived on the east side of town. At that time the more affluent people, black and white, lived on the west side of town.

Our neighborhood was integrated. Blacks, Whites and Mexicans all lived together. Next to our house lived a white fellow by the name of Fred – that's all I ever knew was Fred. But I do know that Fred didn't seem to be like the rest of the white people because Fred was damn sure a wino but he seemed to like me. Maybe it was because I would help him into his little one-bedroom house when he was drunk and passed out in his back yard. Fred would make "little Roy" welcome in his shack anytime I wanted to go see him. I became fascinated by the magazines that he read. At that time John Dillinger, Bonnie Parker and Clyde Barrow, Machine Gun Kelly, Pretty Boy Floyd, Ma Barker, Baby Face Nelson and a host of other gangsters and outlaws were making headlines in the newspapers, movie newsreels and magazines, and I would read every magazine that Fred had about these people. It was an outlet for me at that time I guess. Anyway, Fred was my buddy. I suppose it was because he took time with a kid when other grown-ups didn't have the time to. I never did know what he did for a living or how he made it, but I do know he always had his wine.

In the summertime we used to have a garden with corn, tomatoes, carrots, cucumbers, onions, cabbage, greens, etc., and Mom always kept a few chickens, but our backyard was not fenced in. The chickens were kept in a chicken coop, naturally, but quite often some of our chickens would be missing. Fred would have me to eat with him sometimes. Mom would ask me, "Roy Lee, what did you and Fred eat at his house?"

I say, "Chicken, mama."

Mom would say, "I know Fred is the one that is stealing our chickens, but he doesn't know I know. Son, you are at Fred's house eating your own chicken." Anyway, I liked Fred. When Bonnie and Clyde were killed, their 1933 Ford that was riddled with bullets was put on tour across the nation for the public to see. Fred took me with him to see it.

My little sister Evelyn was my favorite little girl and I didn't want anyone messing with her, but she was always bugging me to hang with big brother. Now you know I couldn't have that, because what I might be into, I damn sure didn't want her to come home and tell Mom. Dig? Evelyn had a temper and would get into fights with the other girls but it was a long time before she ever won any fights. Instead, she would run. One day Mom was watering the grass in the front yard and looked up, and here comes Evelyn running so fast from another girl that she ran past home. The other girl was right behind her. I got tired of that and told Evelyn if she didn't stop running from fights that I would kick her ass myself. The girl's name was Peaches. She kicked Peaches's ass good and didn't have any more trouble. I think after that she thought she was tough.

Mom had said she wasn't going to marry again because she "didn't want no other man over my children." That was silly and I told her so because old man Muldrow liked her and I liked old man Muldrow, plus he was a good carpenter. Yet she never remarried. I can't recall how or when Mom first met Mr Muldrow. I know he came to our house to do some carpentry or plumbing work. It was obvious he had eyes for Mom because he was always volunteering his services. Mr Muldrow didn't have a shop of his own; instead he worked out of his home. He was a nice man and seemed to like Evelyn and me. He was short, which may have turned Mom off, since he was not as tall as my Dad.

On my unpaved, graveled street, Frank Trujillo, a Mexican, lived two houses from me and Vernon Austin and his brother, white boys, lived diagonally across the street. We went to school together, shot marbles, played cowboy, cops and robbers and all the traditional things that kids do. We would fight, call each other names. Vernon would call me a nigger, I would call him a peckerwood, Frank would call me a nigger, I would call him a greaser, but we would end up playing together. Still, in the movie theatres Blacks had to sit in the balcony. I couldn't fathom the reason then because we all went to the same schools. This was not the South or a big city with a ghetto, but even at that early age I could still feel deep inside me the different levels of acceptance between the races.

My childhood was by no means stormy or what you would call bad. By comparison with many black kids in the South or some large cities in the East, I had it fairly good. The schools were integrated, which meant you could get the same education, but the restaurants, hotels, theaters, etc., weren't. I was enrolled in Helen Hunt Elementary School and there my formal education as a child actually began. In the classrooms you sat and studied together, but at the school dances Blacks and Whites "just didn't" dance together. So I grew up not wanting to hear that shit about all things being equal.

One day while still at Helen Hunt we were playing baseball and I was batting. A white kid was standing to my left, and when I swung the bat I missed the ball and the bat flew out of my hands, hitting this kid in the head. All hell broke loose as if I had done it on purpose. There was a fight, but only I was expelled, no one else. I knew something wasn't right, but still couldn't understand why.

After what little money my father had left was gone, my mother, with only a third-grade education, had to take in washing and ironing, plus work as a domestic in the homes of white people. But she was determined that her children would get an education. I was the man of the house then, so on weekends I sold newspapers downtown on street corners until I was able to buy a raggedy bicycle for eight dollars. This enabled me to build up a pretty good paper route so I could make a little more change.

With my paper route and ice and coal route, I was able to get through school and help my mom a little financially. The railroad tracks were not too far from where I lived and I could see the freight trains come in with the refrigerated cars and coal cars. I'd get gunny sacks, take my wheelbarrow or wagon, and go throw the coal off the cars, fill up the sacks, put 'em on my wagon and sell 'em to my coal customers. Anthracite was 50 cents a sack. Bituminous, 25 cents a sack. Anthracite is the shiny black hard coal, considered the best because it burns longer. Bituminous is dull black and soft. Naturally, it's cheaper.

In the summertime, the refrigerator cars would be setting there, some with produce, some empty. If the seal on the door of the car was not broken, it meant it was full of produce. If the seal had been broken, that meant it had already been unloaded and there wasn't anything but ice in the car, so it was available. I would climb to the top of these cars, go down into the ice compartment, throw out the blocks of ice, put 'em on my wagon and split. In those days only people of means had refrigerators. My customers had 50¢ size ice boxes and 25¢ ice boxes. A nice little hustle if you didn't get caught.

My mother was a Seventh-Day Adventist, who believed that music was "of this world." But she liked the sound Benny Goodman had on clarinet, so she bought me a cheap Albert system clarinet, sewed a cloth case together for carrying it and allowed me to take lessons at school. I did that for a while, but clarinet wasn't my thing. While she was enjoying Benny Goodman and his clarinet, I was listening to the drummer in the band, Gene Krupa. This is around 1935 and 1936. The kids would make fun of me with that little home-made sack with a clarinet in it and we would go to war many times, but it would always be me that got expelled. That's when I first started to feel racism.

But what capped the feeling and made me know racism was an incident involving a black boy. People were saying there was going to be a riot. I wasn't hip to a riot. The police were going to black people's homes looking for some black boy that raped a white girl. There was lynch talk. Damn, I couldn't believe that. I had heard and read about lynchings of black people in the southern states, but this was Colorado Springs, Colorado. It was that incident that made me truly aware of this sickness. The white girl was actually going with a black man and got caught. She cried rape, and he had to leave town to avoid a possible lynching. I became even more hostile. It finally blew over but definitely left a bad taste in the mouth of black people in Colorado Springs, which was not considered a southern city.

I entered junior high school in September of 1936 and went out for the track team, on which I ran the 50-yard dash and the 100-yard dash and was also an anchor man on the 220 relay team. In the meantime I was still shooting marbles, playing cowboy with my black, white and Mexican buddies and beating on pots and pans. In school I took lessons on the clarinet. But about all I learned in those music classes was the C scale, because my mind was not on any formal training of music. I really liked the drums and at that time very few drummers in swing bands knew how to read music. I was interested in track, playing the drums, and girls, in that order.

Our home was far from a mansion. We couldn't afford gas heating in the house so we burned coal in a pot-bellied stove in the living room and a coal-burning stove in the kitchen for cooking. Our toilet was out on the back porch and we had to bathe in galvanized tubs. We would heat the water in buckets on the kitchen stove, pour it into the tub and take our bath. I didn't know what a shower was. When you used the toilet on the back porch in the winter time you froze your ass off. Sometimes it would be 15 or 20 degrees below zero. But the more affluent homes had nice bathrooms inside and had gas heating. We were not that fortunate, but there was love in our home.

The luxuries of our house were an old upright piano, a small radio that sat on top of the piano and later, when we could afford it, a telephone. Having a piano around was how I was able to pick out melodies and chords and learn how to play boogie-woogies. I used to hear Albert Ammons and Meade "Lux" Lewis on the radio and do them by ear.

The little radio sitting on top of the piano cleared up some things about my future. On Saturday nights I would hear the swing bands broadcasting from New York, Chicago, Philadelphia, etc. I would hear Benny Goodman; Glenn Miller, from the Pennsylvania Hotel; Tommy Dorsey, Jan Savitt from Philadelphia; Glen Gray and the Casa Loma Orchestra from the Glen Island Casino in Atlantic City and more: all white bands on the prime-time radio broadcasts.

Meantime, after the Goodmans, Dorseys, Millers, etc., broadcasts would go off the air, once in a while you could hear Jimmie Lunceford, Count Basie and Erskine Hawkins's bands from the Savoy Ballroom in Harlem or Duke Ellington and Earl Hines from the Grand Terrace Ballroom in Chicago. I also heard Chick Webb's band with Ella Fitzgerald doing their hit *A-tisket A-tasket* and Chick's famous drum solo *Liza* that made me even more determined to play drums. I was still taking lessons on clarinet, plink-planking on the piano and beating on anything available – pots, pans, the stove, the bed, walls and logs, which gave me the idea to try and make a drum.

I got an old Crisco can, stretched some heavy meat-packing paper over it, tightened it with a strong rubber band, made some home-made sticks and started working on some Gene Krupa licks, because they were simple rudiments and were easy. My mother said, "Boy if you don't quit beating that noise, I'll kill you." She got tired of that shit, so I ended up with a cheap bass drum, snare drum, foot pedal, small crash cymbal, sticks and brushes from the one and only music store in town, Colorado Springs Music Company.

Man, I thought I was bad. Mom was disappointed because she wanted me to play clarinet in church for the Lord, bless her soul. She even wanted me to play the drums for the Lord. I never did know why, because the Seventh-Day Adventist church sure wasn't a Holy Roller church. I regret that mother never lived long enough to see or hear me play professionally. That saddens me.

Mom was lovable, kind, courteous and all those good

things, but she believed in that "turn the other cheek" philosophy a little too much. We walked about 20 blocks to church every Saturday morning. There was an automobile repair shop situated on the street and we had to pass it every Sabbath morning. On our little journey to praise the Lord, every time we passed the garage these crackers would say derogatory remarks such as, "Hey Aunt Jemima, how ya'll pickaninnies doin'?" and laugh. I would see red every time that shit would happen.

I asked my mother why she didn't say anything back and she would say, "Son, the Lord teaches us to turn the other cheek," and we would keep walking. I said to myself, "Shit, I'm going to have to put a stop to this." At this time I was about 11 or 12 years old. The next Saturday on our way to praise the Lord, the same thing happened. I stopped and looked at this big redneck and said, "Why don't you leave us alone you peckerwood motherfucker?" When we got home from church, Mama took a branch off a tree and whipped my ass good. I asked, "Why are you whipping me, Mama? I get tired of those men always messin' with us."

She said, "Son, those words can't hurt us. Just ignore them. I'm whipping you because you used curse words." I should have known better, because I was building a go-cart one time earlier and hit my finger with a hammer and she heard me say, "Goddamit."

She called, "Roy Lee, come in here," and beat my butt. But at least those dudes didn't keep that same shit up every Saturday morning.

Mom, being a strict and avid Seventh-Day Adventist, was at first apprehensive about the music idea. When I would play boogie-woogie on piano she would say, "Boy, why do you play that noise? Play some of the Lord's music." Church music didn't give me that same feeling it gave other people. Like even today, people are always talking about how gospel and church music moves them. That's alright, but I don't dig no "hoopin' and hollerin' and moanin'," or even "We Shall Overcome Someday," which is still really begging for justice that is rightfully ours anyway.

Our family went to the only Seventh-Day Adventist church in Colorado Springs. It was white, but we were the only Blacks that were Seventh-Day Adventists there, so we were tolerated. My sister and I were both baptized in the Seventh-Day Adventist church. The Seventh-Day Adventists are a denomination that believes that the seventh day of the week is the Sabbath. We went to Sabbath School, as opposed to Sunday School, and church services on Saturday. On that day you did nothing but worship until the sun set. That meant when the sun went down on Friday, it was the beginning of the Sabbath. Their belief is that the beginning of the next day is at sunset, not 12 midnight. All worldly things such as housework, cooking, chores and baths must be finished by sundown. We didn't eat pork, lard, coffee, use tobacco, drink alcohol, dance or eat any meat from animals referred to in Leviticus, Chapter 11, of the Bible.

So it was somewhat surprising that I became a musician at all, as it is "of the world," and my mom didn't believe in worldly things. My mind was in a dilemma about this for quite some time then.

At about this same time, I began beating drums with the McDonalds' family band. It consisted of Mr McDonald Sr, tuba; Max, trombone and piano; John, trumpet and piano; and myself, drums. We worked Friday and Saturday nights at the local black dance hall, Douglas Hall. It was rented out on Friday night for Mexicans and on Saturday night for Blacks. On holidays such as Christmas, New Year's Eve, Fourth of July and Easter we were quite busy, especially New Year's Eve, when we played the classy Broadmoor Hotel for the white millionaires. We went in through the servants' entrance to play music for them. Even at that age I felt one of the solutions to the human rights problem just might be music, because it brought a certain amount of respect from even your adversaries. Little did I know then that plenty of storms lay ahead in my musical life.

By hearing Lunceford, Basie, Earl Hines and other black bands on the radio, I was finally able to distinguish the difference between white music and black music. I would hear Budd Johnson on tenor sax solos with Earl Hines's band and Tex Beneke on sax with Glenn Miller, and it was a world of difference in feeling and soul. The same was true with Chick Webb and Gene Krupa or Big Sid Catlett and Buddy Rich on drums. Don't get me wrong, the white bands were sounding good ensemble- and arrangement-wise, but the feeling wasn't the same. White bands were, note for note, so precise and tight. The black bands were loose and swinging. One of the best white bands of that era was Jan Savitt and his Top-Hatters out of Philadelphia. They swung pretty good and were the first white band I heard with a black male vocalist. His name was Bon Bon Tunnell, who had a big hit of the day called *It's a Wonderful World*.

The big-name white bands would play one-nighters in Colorado Springs at the Broadmoor Hotel, the Antlers Hotel, and a ballroom called the Hiawatha Gardens in Manitou, but I couldn't go inside. I remember standing outside and listening to Jan Savitt when he played there.

George Morrison, Hoggy Harper and Kenny "Sticks" McVey, all black musicians from Denver who had their own bands, would occasionally come down to the Springs and play dances at Douglas Hall. Still, very seldom would a big-name band come to Colorado Springs. But I did get to hear Nat Towles's and Lloyd Hunter's black territorial bands either in the Springs or in Pueblo. They were very good bands out of Omaha, Nebraska, but they were semi-names, so when a name band came to either Pueblo or Denver all the people would get in cars and drive to the dances there.

The big-name black bands such as Earl Hines would skip Colorado Springs and play Pueblo or Denver. Everyone would play Denver's Rainbow Ballroom. That's where I first saw Louis Armstrong's big band with Big Sid Catlett on drums. Armstrong came to Denver to play the Rainbow Ballroom one Saturday night. Me and my buddy Leroy Kirven put on our zoot suits, put some coveralls over our togs, caught the freight train to Denver and heard Louis Armstrong's big band. Armstrong himself didn't especially move me, but watching Sid Catlett play convinced me that I definitely wanted to play drums professionally. He was such a big man with so much finesse, especially with brushes, so smooth and clean: my main man. I didn't meet him that night because I didn't have the nerve to say hello. He didn't even know I was there. Later I met him in New York City.

Denver was a city of about 75,000 population at that time, so you know much more was happening in the Mile High City than in little Colorado Springs. It had hip places like the Rossonian Hotel, Benny Hooper's After Hours Club and a few more clubs all located on the Five Points. The Points are where five streets meet like the spokes of a wheel. Welton Street, Washington Street, 26th Avenue, 25th Street and Tremont Avenue all come together at one intersection in the black neighborhood of Denver.

After the dance we went down to Five Points to an after-hours place called Benny Hooper's on Welton Street. We couldn't get in because we were too young, but that is where all the musicians would hang out and jam. So, we waited outside, listening. Finally, me and Leroy went back to the freight yard where we had stashed our coveralls, put 'em on, caught another freight going south and hoboed on back to Colorado Springs. We had done the same thing earlier to hear Earl Hines in Pueblo. We were drinking port wine and smoking pot and we hoboed to Denver and Pueblo many times to see some hot-to-trot foxes. It was a ball, especially at the ages of 14, 15 and 16.

In 1936 the Great Depression was really hitting the country, but at that age it didn't really dawn on me what was happening. President Franklin Delano Roosevelt had something going called the New Deal. I remember well the WPA (Work Projects Administration) and the CCC (Civilian Conservation Corps) camps which provided people with work.

The Depression really didn't bother us because we were poor people anyway. On Thanksgiving and Christmas we were able to go to the Salvation Army and get the traditional holiday baskets of foodstuffs. Also the federal government had a relief program that provided staple foods such as powdered milk, butter, flour, rice, beans, etc., to poor families, and there were plenty of them. But I can truthfully say that I was never hungry or cold.

I was still telling my mother that it would be alright for her to marry again as far as my sister and I were concerned. She was still saying, "I don't want no other man over my children." My mom was beautiful. I suppose she still loved Dad. Bless her soul, she wasn't around but a few years after that.

I was a C-average student at South Junior High, and was the fastest 50- and 100-yard dash man in my weight class in Colorado Springs. There were two other junior high schools in town and, at the end of the track season, South Junior, West Junior and North Junior met at Washburn Field for the City Track and Field Championship. All three years of my junior high terms I won either first or second place in the dashes. Boy, I'd strut like a peacock wearing my letter and ribbons on my sweater. In 1936 Jesse Owens had set the world record at 9.4 seconds at the Olympics. In the ninth grade, I was doing it in 10.2 seconds.

My first year of high school, 1939, I was still doing my little thing on drums but I was teaching myelf. I organized my own band and we would play for some of the functions at assembly or a program in the auditorium at school, but I noticed when prom night came they would hire a white band that was worse than we were. I never understood that, but I hadn't given up my little gig with the McDonalds, so it was alright.

I had organized my own little band with guys that were in high school with me. These guys just wanted something to do in their spare time, not seriously at all. Of the members of that band, John Childress, the piano player, became a printing instructor at Dorsey High School. Bill McNulty, a real bookworm that played the saxophone, probably is a professor at Yale. The rest, I don't know, but I do know I became a professional without the formal musical training that I should have taken advantage of. My unfortunate attitude about formal musical education continued at Wiley College and all through my career until Chino.

At high school my mom finally did get to see me play for the first and only time. We had to play on a talent program in the school auditorium and it was a very critical situation because it was on a Friday night, the Sabbath. I finally persuaded her to sin this one time and come to see her son at a worldly function. This is about the only sin that I know of my mother committing. But I am glad because she finally did get an opportunity to see and hear me play those drums that had given her many "headaches" over the years. Most of all she enjoyed it because it was her son.

In the ninth grade I began smoking pot. They called it reefer then. I was drinking red port wine, which was called Loney Doney. I was playing with older musicians at the age of 13 and would drink right along with them. One of the reasons I didn't go out for the track team when I got to high school was because of playing music weekends and drinking wine and smoking reefers. My buddy Leroy Kirven and I would pick up a joint from a dude we knew and stand under the viaduct or walk on the rails in the railroad yard and get high. I suppose I became chemically dependent at an early age.

My mother never did get hip to that as far as I know, but she did smell wine on my breath a few times and took a strap and beat my ass good. I might have been a track star if I had pursued it, but I had gotten interested in playing music.

When I started high school in 1939, I was still playing with the McDonalds' band, in which I learned a lot. I was able to play *Sing, Sing, Sing* and *Drumboogie*, Gene Krupa's famous drum solos from Benny Goodman's records. I was also getting proficient at faking the drum parts of the stock arrangements we sometimes played. The people of my home town thought I was great, but I knew there wasn't anything happening with my playing. My loyal fans, however, didn't. They were beautiful people and I will never forget them. They thought I was a phenomenon.

At the time there was only one high school in the city and I decided not to go out for the school track team because of my drinking wine and smoking pot. I knew I wouldn't be able to train properly. Playing music became my main goal. I was doing well academically in typing, shorthand, history, English, geography and print shop class.

My teacher in printing class, Mr Harold L. Mahnke, was impressed with my typesetting and suggested I pursue printing or journalism in college. Out of all the teachers at school, I remember him best. He seemed to really care that you learned in class, regardless of race. He encouraged my interest in journalism when I graduated. He knew I had good grades in Gregg shorthand and typing and seemed to take a special interest in me. He was well aware of my interest in playing music and liked my little high-school band and thought I was a terrific "drum beater." I have always remembered Harold L. Mahnke. Once, sad to say, I got into a fight in his classroom and felt so bad. He was my favorite instructor in Colorado Springs High School.

I also recall all of the chicks, white and black, that were ready. But a white chick and a black dude getting together was nil. That unwritten law could be seen, heard and felt everywhere, even in Colorado, which is considered a northern state. Yeah, you could sneak if you wanted to, but even as a teenager I felt that if you had to do that, then you would lose your dignity as a man.

A musician could damn near get any girl he wanted – white, black, brown, red or yellow. You were looked up to if you played an instrument. If you were good, you'd have to beat broads back with a stick.

Even at that age young chicks, older broads and even old women liked me. But the older ones taught me what was happening in life about relationships between male and female. I won't print some of the things that older women taught me sexually. It did tighten my skull as far as knowing what to do with or for a female, good or bad. All of this prepared me for certain escapades or situations that happened to and for me, all during my career in music. I have known some fantastic females.

In my last year of junior high school I was taught by an older woman that, in my career, I would be pursued by women that wanted to do things for me and to take advantage of them, so I guess I became spoiled in that respect. But it was true. I respected her for telling me the working of the female mind, but she only told me because she knew I had to grow into manhood and would inevitably learn the same thing sooner or later. I give her laurels and respect for being so direct with me. I suppose her motives for giving me this information was that I would give her recognition later for this invaluable advice. And I do.

I will never forget Coletta (that's not her real name). She was two years older than I was and had dropped out of high school, but, baby, you talk about a fox with a gorgeous black face, big pretty titties, slim waist, beautiful ass and big pretty hairy legs. She was a hirsute chick with hair from her navel all down to her ankles. Every man, boy, girl and woman wanted Coletta because she was just that bad. She lived on the west side of town and I had to go through Monument Park to get to her house. We would wait until her parents and the rest of her family were in bed and "get it on" in the living room on the couch. In the summertime we would go to Monument Park and get it on under some low-branched pine trees, bushes, or out in the cornfield in my backyard. Coletta was a monster, so fine that a piano player who came through Colorado Springs with a touring band out of New Orleans married her and took her to Los Angeles. She became a famous beauty queen in LA and Hollywood. But Coletta made me know how powerful being able to play music made an individual, even in junior high and high school. I give women the credit for letting me know a lot of things about life at that early age that otherwise I wouldn't have known.

Colorado Springs High had an 84-piece marching band, 70-piece orchestra, track team, football team, basketball, tennis and a golf squad. But there were only two Blacks in the band, the orchestra or the sports teams: Van Saunders on the track team and Aletha Woods in the violin section of the orchestra. In fairness, though, there wasn't but a few black kids at school and there was only a very sparse population of Blacks in the city. I didn't play in either the band or the orchestra, mainly because of tension and sensitivity on my part. Another reason was that I was playing semi-professionally and making a little piece of money on the side. I guess I have always been a maverick.

There were two older drummers in Colorado Springs which I admired and who were a source of pride and inspiration to me. They were either brothers or cousins, I was never sure: Eugene and Percy Stanley. Gene was the first trick drummer I saw. He would throw his sticks up in the air, twirl them behind his back and catch them with his teeth, all while he played, à la Lionel Hampton. I had never seen this done before and to me it was very exciting. He finally moved to Denver and died some years ago. Percy, if he is still with us, is still in Colorado Springs. He was the first drummer that I saw that played left-handed or what I call side-saddle drums. He was a much better drummer music-wise than Gene. He worked many years with a saxophonist named John "Fez" Bryant.

John was famous among the white people in the Springs as he also worked as janitor at Colorado Springs Music Store. Everyone knew him and he was very popular. His group worked at a roadhouse on the outskirts of town on the highway to Denver, as a duo, sax and drums. They'd probably still be there now if John Bryant had not died in 1974. The McDonalds' band and John Bryant were the only two black bands in the Springs.

A bit later, in 1939 or 1940, Earl Hines came back through Pueblo, 45 miles south of the Springs, to play a one-nighter dance. Here we go again. Me and Leroy Kirven get sharp, put coveralls over our sharpness, jump in a boxcar on the freight train and hobo to Pueblo. Once there we stashed our coveralls in the freight yard and walked to the dance. Now I was getting a pretty good reputation in Denver and Pueblo. People would be saying, "You heard that youngster from Colorado Springs? He sure can whip them drums, chile." We got to the dance and some of the people knew who I was so they started asking Earl Hines's road manager to let me play. I said to myself, "These people are crazy, I'm never going to be good enough to play in a band like this." Earl Hines's band was up there on the bandstand, burning. Pretty soon the road manager said I could play a few licks at intermission. At intermission I got to the drums and didn't know where to start, because those drums were big-time drums compared to my little high-school set. I would have done better if I had been able to adjust the seat, snare drum and cymbals position-wise, but I didn't know if that would be the right thing to do, so I didn't.

I was shy and nervous anyway. I had never been on anyone's bandstand in the presence of people like Earl Hines's band. I was shaking like a leaf, but I picked up a pair of mallets and started playing Gene Krupa's *Sing, Sing, Sing* on the big floor tom tom. Then I switched to sticks, played some triplets accented different ways, switched to brushes and ended up back with the mallets. I guess I played maybe five minutes. Man, the people in the audience thought I was good. The guys in the band knew better, however, and didn't say shit to me. I knew better, too. I didn't know who the guys were in Hines's band because I didn't meet anyone. Truthfully, I was embarrassed because, even though the public was clamoring for more, I didn't get the respect of my peers.

I learned a valuable lesson that night. On the way home in the freight car I made up my mind that I had to get away from my home town of Colorado Springs if I was ever going to be a musician of any substance at all.

I was almost 18 years old and my sister Evelyn was almost 14. When I told Mom I wanted to go off to college, she understood every word I was saying and said, "Son, that is what I have lived for, my children's education. Go and try and do good and great things in your lifetime, but always remember the Lord." Mom was an angel. I graduated from Colorado Springs High School in June of 1941.

On one of my previous trips to Denver I had met Paul

Quinichette, the tenor saxophonist, who lived there. We met on a trip to Denver to hear Kenny "Sticks" McVey, a drummer I admired. We were discussing colleges and he said he was going to enrol at Tennessee State College and how nice it would be if we could go to the same school. I had been corresponding with two or three schools, including Tennessee State, but I had heard and read so much about the Wiley Collegians' College Band that I chose Wiley. I didn't see Paul Quinichette again, as our paths never crossed in the musical world.

When I graduated from high school in 1941, Camp Carson, an army base, was under construction as war was inevitable. I had decided to enrol at Wiley College, so my buddy Leroy Kirven decided to attend Bishop College, a Baptist college also in Marshall, Texas. So we got serious about making some money for school in September. We went out to Camp Carson looking for any kind of job. The man said, "Boys, about the only job you can do here is keep the toilets supplied with toilet paper and be water boys for the construction workers. Do you want it or not?" We said yes. We worked that summer and made enough money for train fare to Marshall, Texas.

In September of 1941 we boarded the train at the Santa Fe railroad station, drums, trunk, and suitcase. We said "Adios" to Colorado Springs for at least nine months. When I got to the Texas border, the Mason–Dixon line, and had to move to a segregated car in the back, belongings and all, I said, "Aw Goddamn, what kind of shit have I gotten myself into now?" But we rolled right on to one of the most pleasurable and rewarding events of my life.

3

Wiley College

When I arrived in Marshall, Texas, in September of 1941 I took a cab from the train station to Wiley College. Immediately I sensed that the students were wondering, "Who is this dude with all these raggedy ass drums?" Wiley at that time had a reputation as a very prestigious private black Methodist institution.

After leaving my drums and gear at the men's dormitory I was directed to the registrar's office and then to the president's office, Dr William Dogan. At first he looked at me rather strangely, but then I could see amazement and compassion in his eyes. After some time, he finally asked, "Are you the young man from Colorado that has been writing about attending this school?"

I said, "Yes sir. I came here to study journalism and play drums in the Wiley Collegians' band, sir."

He kindly replied, "But, son, we already have a drummer who is on full scholarship just for that purpose, but this is his last year." My eyes filled with tears, and I said to myself, "Damn! I came all this way for nothing." But still I wanted with all my heart and soul to attend Wiley College. He took another look at me, saw how disappointed I was and said, "Young man, if you had the desire and nerve to come all the way from Colorado out here to Marshall, Texas, for an education, then you *will* go to school. But, son, you will have to work for your tuition."

For a while there I must have been one of the happiest waiters in the campus dining hall. After a bit I got to know Ruth Brownlee, President Dogan's secretary, who was a cute little fox. Eventually I ended up working as her assistant in her office since I could type and do filing work. I'll never forget the kindnesses of President Dogan and Miss Brown-lee.

That first semester Eddie Preston and I were roommates. He too was waiting tables in the dining room. McKinley Dorham was washing pots and pans in the kitchen at that point, but none of us were in the college band yet.

The Wiley Collegians were under the direction of Mr Bertrand Adams, a trombonist. Throughout my freshman year he held closed rehearsals at night in the dining hall. So, Eddie Preston, Kinney Dorham and I would sit outside and listen. Finally, Mr Adams invited us to come in and listen. Man, that band was just as hot as most big-name profes-sional bands. I was eventually asked if I wanted to sit in, although I believe it was mostly a case of them thinking, "Let's get this dude out of our hair." I really don't think they thought I could play those arrangements. But shit, I knew those arrangements from A to Z since I had sat outside for so long. I played all of the arrangements plus a drum solo. After that I was able to travel with the band as a featured solo drummer for the rest of my freshman year.

The big band in 1941 included Bill Gillohm, Eddie Preston, Russell Jacquet and Volley Bastine, trumpets (Kinney Dorham didn't make the band the first year); Hosea Martin and Richard Waters, trombones; James Braxton, Robert Braxton, Roy Roberts, Edward Pennigar and Billy Frazier, saxophones; Louis Inghram, bass; William "Wild Bill" Davis, piano and arranger; and myself on drums. William Banks, the band's regular drummer, had to leave school for the army, so the position was mine. One person I can't forget is Grady Orange who did all of the band's vocals. Grady Orange later became a famous physician in Los Angeles.

That was a hell of a band. The Wiley Collegians were so good that we played most of the black college proms throughout the area. We played all over the South at places like Prairie View College, Texas College and Bishop College in Texas, Xavier University in Louisiana, Langston Uni-versity in Oklahoma, and many more. We'd also have a battle of the bands every year in Houston, Texas, with Milton Larkin's big band. Milton Larkin's band was outrageous with greats like Arnett Cobb, Eddie "Cleanhead" Vinson, Illinois Jacquet and, as arranger and featured pianist, Cedric Haywood.

The first time I caught Cat Anderson, the phenomenal trumpet player who went on to create such a stir with Duke Ellington, we were having a battle of the bands with the Carolina Cotton Pickers at the Regal nightclub in Dallas. Now, the Carolina Cotton Pickers were famous for their screaming high-tone trumpet section – quite a strong band. But the Wiley Collegians "romped" right on through them, and they were all professionals.

Wiley also had good football and basketball teams. When the football team would play other colleges over the weekend the marching band and the Wiley Collegians would travel with the team and play half-time shows and then play the dance that night.

Every Thanksgiving Day Wiley's football team would play Prairie View in the Cotton Bowl in Dallas. The Cotton Bowl always had sporting events such as football there, and it was the bowl that the Dallas Cowboys first played when they organized their franchise. College teams, both black and white in the State of Texas, would use the bowl for their games on Saturdays and holidays. During half time the marching bands played and put on great shows. The "after the game" dances were open to the public and were usually held at the Pythian Temple or the Rose Room. These were ballrooms that professional bands and entertainers were booked into. At that time, the Wiley Collegians took great pride in being just as professional, both musically and appearance-wise, as most professional big-name bands. During the football season our dances would have as many people as the ballrooms would hold. It was quite a thrill to play in such an environment.

During this time, while down at the Rose Room in Dallas, I heard the fine orchestra of Harlan Leonard's called the Kansas City Rockets. That was the first time that I got to see in person one of my favourite drummers, the great Jesse Price.

In the 1940s Texas was a "dry" state and no booze could

legally be sold. So we had to get "skag" from the bootleg-
gers. Skag was a nickname for the bootleg whiskey that the
moonshiners sold. It was of varying potencies and was
distilled from local crops. That shit would knock your ass to
the ground, especially if you mixed it with nutmeg.

I first got turned on to the nutmeg kick at Wiley. You'd
buy a can of nutmeg and mix it with a Coca-Cola and you'll
get a light buzz, but mix it with that moonshine or white
lightning whiskey which they were making and you got a
great big buzz. This was great fun, especially when we
would sneak chicks out of Dogan Hall, the girls' dormitory,
at night and get it on. The men's dorm was named Coe Hall
and was located on the other side of the campus. In between
Dogan and Coe was the administration building, the various
classrooms, the dining hall, and the gymnasium. A dude
called Moon was the night watchman, but, for all of his
smiles, Moon would kick your ass if you were caught
slipping any of those fine women into Coe Hall. But Moon
really wasn't able to keep up with all of our antics.

I had a ball going to Wiley because I had previously only
been to integrated schools in Colorado. It was a good feeling
being at an all-black school. Having never been to the South
before, I found the only difference at that time between
North and South was that you could vote in the northern
states and there were no "Colored Only" or "White Only"
signs in the integrated public schools in the North. Other
than that the old attitudes remained in both places and I just
didn't see much difference.

I also got turned on to Juneteenth Day. June 19th is
celebrated by the black community, particularly in the
southern states, because the Emancipation Proclamation
which abolished slavery was signed into law on 19 June
1862. It is celebrated just like the Fourth of July as
Independence Day. In Colorado I had never heard of
Juneteenth and no form of black history was taught in the
public schools there.

Kinney Dorham, Eddie Preston, James Braxton and I were
all jamming in our dorm the morning of 7 December 1941

when President Roosevelt announced over the radio that Pearl Harbor had been bombed. After that, in order to remain in school, all students of draft age had to enlist in the Army Reserves to be able to continue their education. This meant that technically you were in the army but as long as you stayed in school and kept your grades up you would not be drafted.

I enlisted on 12 December 1941 in Tyler, Texas. By this time my major had changed from journalism to music and most of my energies were focused on the band. I'll admit that all I was there for was to play in the Wiley Collegians band.

But I did get the chance to pursue my study of journalism for several months, since I became a reporter for the school paper, the *Wiley Reporter*. The paper was a small campus newsletter which appeared monthly. It was operated strictly by journalism students under the direction of Ms Pearson, senior editor and professor of literature. The remainder of the staff were students who acted as campus reporters. There was someone who covered sports events and someone else wrote a gossip column. I reported various anecdotes about the Wiley Collegians and their travels when we were out on the road playing proms and public dances. All monies made at such events were always used for the Wiley College Scholarship Fund. At that time, Wiley was a small, tightly knit college and so whatever happened to our classmates was generally regarded as a big thing and was duly reported as such.

Many of the professors at Wiley were quite encouraging to me as a young student. In addition to Ms Pearson, who encouraged my aptitude for journalism and helped secure a job on the campus paper for me, there were such other notables as Professor Smith, from whom I learned a few words of German; Professors Tolson and Edmondson, who both knew I would never make it in math; Professor Lewis, the black history and English teacher, whom I admired because he was himself at all times, even when he did come to class full of skag; Dr Morris, the chemistry teacher, who knew I was not interested in his class; and my main man,

Professor William Henry Smith, the choir director and music theory teacher. Professor Smith frequently allowed me to snatch Homoselle LaVerne Davis, my main squeeze on campus, and let me walk her back to Dogan Hall. As I have mentioned, I greatly admired Bertrand Adams as both leader and director of the Wiley Collegians. Interestingly enough, the dean of the men's dormitory was his wife, Hazel Poole Adams. She was a big, pretty-legged lady, who was a stunner on campus, but ran the dorm as efficiently as any man. She was also the physical education instructor for the women.

When June of 1942 rolled around I headed home to Colorado Springs. There I spent the summer saving money for another year at Wiley by playing gigs around town. I also worked out at Peterson Field Air Base, which was being built east of town. There I was still carrying toilet paper for the workers' toilets and being a waterboy. But I saved enough money to go back to school and come September I was at Wiley again.

My sophomore term I was given a music scholarship to play in the band and so most of the economic pressure was gone. My good friend President Dogan had retired because of poor health. A Dr McCloud had replaced him, and not long after Dr Dogan died.

Bertrand Adams had left so Wild Bill Davis became the bandleader of the Collegians. Eddie Preston didn't return to college and his trumpet chair was taken by Kinney Dorham from Austin, Texas. There were quite a few changes that second year, but the band was still one of the baddest college bands in the country.

Bill Davis would take a Jimmie Lunceford or Earl Hines record, play it once and transcribe the arrangement. I've never seen anyone else with his gift and he remains one of the great arrangers of all time. He'll always be remembered for that famous *April in Paris* arrangement he did for Basie which won a Grammy.

Kinney Dorham and I were roommates our sophomore year and during our first term back our man Moon caught us slipping chicks into our dorm room. There was no ass kicking, but we almost got sent home. We probably would have if we hadn't been in the college band.

The Wiley Collegians played all over the state of Texas: Houston, Dallas, Fort Worth, Port Arthur, Beaumont, Tyler, Midland and some places I'd never heard of before like Nacogdoches and Waxahachie. I remember getting very excited when it was announced that we were soon to play Paris. When I heard that I said, "Damn, we bad. We goin' to France!" Shit, Paris, Texas, wasn't even that far from Marshall, Texas.

On one of our dances I met Floyd Smith, one of the greatest guitarists of the day. He came out of Andy Kirk's band but was stationed at that time in the army in Texas. That was memorable, but there were really so many great musicians from Texas and Oklahoma.

I had heard of southern hospitality before, but I didn't really know what it meant until I started attending Wiley. Everywhere the band played the people were so friendly. When the band hit town, especially the small towns, the people were always right there to greet you with a, "Do you have a place to stay?" or, "Come on over to the house and have some dinner." And they really meant it. These were soulful, kind people. Southern people are sincere. If they liked you or your music you were treated as a celebrity.

In Texarkana we were playing a dance one night and we were sounding great. Texarkana is a city that is half in Texas and half in Arkansas. And at this time Texas, Louisiana and Oklahoma were all dry states. But after the dance a group of people took us over to the Arkansas side of town, loaded up our bus with cases of whiskey, beer and wine and said, "This is for playin' so good at our dance." Boy, if we had been stopped by the police probably the whole bus-load would have been thrown in jail for smuggling.

It has always been popular for black bands to play for all white dances and other affairs as long as there is no mixing of the races. Then you were treated like a servant, no matter what you were, especially in the South. I personally experienced this treatment when the Wiley Collegians were playing a dance for a white sorority club at the biggest hotel in Marshall, Texas. Some of the sorority sisters were admiring and enjoying our music. A couple of us were invited to their table for a drink and a chat. This didn't last long, however, before one of the white hotel waiters said, "Ya'll have to get up because we don't serve niggers."

I never played an integrated gig in the South. Some time later, Blacks were allowed to be in the balcony and watch white folks dance, but they still couldn't be on the same dance floor.

In March of 1943 I had to leave college because my mother had become gravely ill and had to have a gallstone operation. Not too long after I found myself away from Wiley, I realized that, despite the ups and downs, I had spent some of the happiest, most rewarding days of my life there.

After I was home in Colorado Springs for a while, Milton Larkin sent for me. I joined his band on Easter Sunday night in April of 1943 at the Rhumboogie nightclub on 55th Street, off South Park Boulevard in Chicago. Milton Larkin was reorganizing his band for a national theater tour with T-Bone Walker, the great blues singer and guitarist. I replaced Joe Marshall in the band, and Freddie Simon and Tom Archia replaced Illinois Jacquet and Arnett Cobb. Being the sole provider for my family at this time I began sending money back to my mom and my sister Evelyn.

When I got to Chicago, since I was a country boy I was so square I didn't know what a jitney was. A jitney is a cab that runs up and down a street and will take as many passengers as can be crammed into it. In this case the jitneys ran along South Park Boulevard and also all down Cottage Grove Avenue. As long as the cab didn't turn off its route, you could ride for miles for a dime. I was staying at the DuSable Hotel on Oakwood just off Cottage Grove. I got in a jitney one night and told the guy to take me to the hotel. I noted he grinned when he said OK, but I didn't think too much of it. When we got to the hotel he charged me 50 cents instead of a dime, explaining that he had to turn off the main drag. So, I learned no more "oaky doaks" for me.

At that time Red Saunders was one of the greatest show drummers in the world. I had heard of Red, so when I was in Chicago I got a chance to see him play with his band at the Club DeLisa at 55th and State streets. He was incredible. A lot of people are not aware of this but Joe Williams got his first break working with Red.

In between our theater dates, Milton Larkin played a weekend at the Cotton Club in Cincinnati, Ohio. We also played a one-nighter at a ballroom in Dayton. Just before we arrived in New York, we had a nice experience when we worked a one-nighter in Harrisburg, Pennsylvania, with Ella Fitzgerald. Chick Webb had been featuring Ella before he passed, and her recording of *A-tisket A-tasket* was very big then.

In Detroit I met Lionel "Gates" Hampton, his drummer, George Jenkins, and Dinah Washington at the Paradise Theater, since Hamp's band followed our engagement there. Dinah was so young and fine, didn't swear much and looked like she was right out of church.

We were on tour with T-Bone Walker, who is really the grand-daddy of all the modern blues guitarists. He was really the star of the Milton Larkin show. T-Bone was a monster on blues guitar. I saw women toss money, keys, brassieres and panties at him. Some of them even came up onto the stage to tear his clothes off when he sang his theme song, *In the Evenin'*. T-Bone is the first dude I saw put his guitar behind his head and get down on his knees and sing and play. He started that trend.

Along this tour, the theater circuit consisted of the Regal Theater in Chicago, the Howard Theater in Washington DC, the Royal Theater in Baltimore, and the Paradise Theater in Detroit. We played the Paradise in about May of 1943 and there was a lot of tension in Detroit. Me and a white girlfriend hailed a cab. The cab driver stopped, looked at her and said, "I don't pick up nigger lovers." When we left

Detroit the riot broke out, and by the time we got to New York City riots were in full swing in Harlem. I had never seen anything like that before, being only 19 years old. Shit, here were all these black people destroying their own ghetto. Harlem was going up in flames and it was frightening.

To a certain extent I could understand the frustrations which had brought on these riot situations. Harlem was, after all, owned and operated by Whites at that time. Close to 95 per cent of all businesses were owned by Whites. Even the most famous establishments such as the Hotel Theresa, located a block from the Apollo Theatre on Seventh Avenue and 125th Street, was not catering to a black clientele.

During all of this I was officially in the Army Enlisted Reserves, but I was able to get a deferment to play an Apollo Theatre date. Just around the corner from the Apollo was the Braddock Hotel on 126th Street and Eighth Avenue. There I met many of the great musicians in the hotel lobby and in the bar and grill downstairs. I also made it to Minton's Playhouse, which was owned by Teddy Hill, a musician and former bandleader. Diz recorded a tune called *Hot House* named after Minton's, and that's what it was. Thelonious Monk, Eddie "Lockjaw" Davis and Kenny "Klook" Clarke were on the stand the night I was in there – quite an experience.

Papa Jo Jones was in Minton's another night and I got a chance to talk with him a bit. Papa Jo was asking me what I thought of the new style of playing drums, so I told him the truth. I said that I wasn't quite hip to it, being from the sticks. He just laughed and said, "Don't worry, young man. No one knows anything about drums anyway." That has always stuck in my mind. It was many years before I really understood just what he meant and why he said that to me. Papa Jo was one of the all-time great drummers.

Before we even got to New York I had already heard quite a bit about how cold New Yorkers were supposed to be. For my part, I was treated OK by some, shitty by others. But it was a new experience for me to hit New York from Colorado

Springs, a hick town by comparison. This was the first time Milton Larkin's band had ever been out of Texas, so it was a new experience for many of the other band members too. That band was good enough to get respect at the Apollo Theatre, although having T-Bone Walker on the bill with us sure didn't hurt. I don't know whether Bone had ever been to New York before, but he sure upset the Apollo Theatre!

Everyone that has played the Apollo in Harlem knows about a dude called Puerto Rico. He was the stage manager and ran the talent shows once a week. He liked to play practical jokes, especially on drummers. So when I got there he said, "Man, you got to have a stage screw in front of your bass drum to keep it from slipping and sliding. Go downtown to the drum shop on Broadway and get one." OK, I go downtown, walk into the shop and ask the man at the counter. He tells me, "There ain't no such thing as a stage screw. Ain't you hip to Puerto Rico yet?" Baby, my jaw was stuck out for days. I felt like one of those hicks from the sticks, but after something like that I learned quick. Yet, this was all in fun. Puerto Rico is dead now and everyone whom I know who ever mentions him really misses him.

The Apollo engagement was the only one Milton Larkin played in New York City. After the gig, some of the guys and me went down to "The Street," 52nd Street. Man, I had never seen so many clubs clustered together in one or two blocks before in my life. 52nd Street was known as the street that never slept, and from what I saw this wasn't much of an exaggeration – club after club. There were places like the Three Deuces and the Famous Door on one side of the street. Across the way was the Onyx, Jimmy Ryan's, Leon & Eddie's, the Spotlight Club, and many others. All of these spots were featuring name jazz musicians like Papa Jo, Shadow Wilson, Kenny Clarke, Art Blakey, Big Sid Catlett, Max Roach, Monk, Diz, Bud Powell, Fats Navarro, and one of the greatest trumpet players, Freddie Webster. I met quite a few of these jazz giants during my first trip to New York in 1943, but that was about it. I just talked with them, sat, listened and admired their playing, particularly all of the great drummers whom I caught. What those musicians were playing completely turned me around musically.

I was able to gig at the Village Vanguard in Greenwich Village with Milt Hinton, Hot Lips Page, Water Page, and a trumpet player named Frankie Newton and an alto saxophonist called Horse Collar. I never did catch his real name.

The Braddock Hotel on 126th Street and Eighth Avenue was home from June to August of 1943. I stayed on in New York after the Apollo date and the Braddock proved helpful, since a lot of musicians stayed there and so it was easy to cop a gig there.

The last job I player prior to going into the army was at Camp Unity. This was a communist camp located north of New York City on the Hudson River near Newburgh, New York. I had never heard much about communism before, but I had seen the *Daily Worker* newspaper on the streets of Harlem. Ironically, the gig was a nice job and tided me over until I reported to Camp Upton and army life in the summer. I played in a four-piece group with two horns, piano and drums. The other band members were New Yorkers and we'd play Unity's recreation hall for dances at night. The people there were all talking racial equality and I must admit I didn't hear one derogatory remark or see any incidents while I was there. Still I think all "racial equality" boiled down to there was that the black musicians had to be with white women since there were no black women in the camp. But I got hip to communism a week after I got there. The game seemed to be to make Blacks embrace their philosophy.

Shortly after this incident I received my draft papers. I reported to Camp Upton Military Base on Long Island on 11 August 1943. Most of the black inductees from the northern states were sent to the South for basic training. Boy, those New York dudes flipped out when we got to Keesler Field Air Force Base in Biloxi, Mississippi. They just weren't used to that type of Jim Crow. I saw guys urinate all over themselves, play gay, act crazy, anything to try and get out of that camp. To add insult to injury, black soldiers tried to catch a bus to town on pass, and if the bus driver felt like it they would close the door in your face and drive off and leave your ass standing there. It was a real bitch because all soldiers, black and white, wore the same United States Army uniforms.

Being a part of the segregated armed services, I can't think of one thing that was not degrading to the dignity of the black soldier, male or female. I, however, got a break of sorts. During basic training my appendix burst and I had to have an operation. I was sent home to Colorado Springs for two weeks' sick leave. During this time Mom was very ill from a gall bladder illness, but I did get a chance to see her then. After my operation I was not able to walk erect. When I returned from sick leave to Keesler I was hospitalized again. Eventually, the doctors made the diagnosis that I had been cut too deeply during my appendix operation. So on 4 February 1944 I was given an honorable discharge and a service-connected pension. I was a private and that was all. My career in the army technically ran from 12 December 1941 through 4 February 1944, though, since I had been in the Enlisted Reserve at Wiley College. I never completed basic training and did not get a chance to play in the army band.

At home I spent some time with my mother, but she died in May of 1944 from her gall bladder operation. Sad to say, with what we know today about gallstones due to the advances in medicine, she would still be alive, since those operations are no longer even necessary. This was a traumatic period for me, but at least the Good Lord kept her alive until I returned home.

My sister Evelyn was married by this time and so she went to live with her husband in Detroit. After we settled up with the house and Mom's belongings I stayed around Colorado Springs for about a month playing a few gigs here and there. In May of 1944 I started another adventure in my life when I moved out to Los Angeles.

4

Central Avenue

I arrived in Los Angeles in late May of 1944 and stayed with my half-sister Odessa in Santa Monica. I had no job, so I helped Mr Tom Lewis do gardening work. He was an old man that had been very close to all of the family and did lawns, pruning, planting, etc., for some of the wealthy white people in Santa Monica, Bel Air and Beverly Hills. It was a few months before I got into Los Angeles proper, but I was raring to see just what the city was like. I asked Odessa to take me over and one day we got on the trolley system, which was known as the Red Cars in those days. It took you through Hollywood to downtown Los Angeles, where you could transfer to other streetcars. The streetcar on Fifth Street was called the U Car. When it got to Central Avenue, it turned south on Central and took you all the way to Watts. When you got to Watts at 103rd Street you had to catch another Red Car to get out to Long Beach.

This was a Sunday afternoon and on the streetcar I could hear people like Joe Liggins, Roy Milton and Erskine Hawkins's *After Hours* blaring from jukeboxes in every joint up and down Central Avenue. That was the first music that greeted me in LA. Shit, Los Angeles was jumping. I told sis, "Hell, I'm moving over to LA and get my feet wet. I've got to get me a gig playing my drums. I ain't no fuckin' gardener."

So I put my change together and moved into the Southway Hotel at 51st and Avalon Boulevard. One of the first musicians I met there was Shifty Henry, a trumpet player who had been at Prairie View College in Texas when I was in Wiley College. Shifty knew who I was and soon we became tight. He said, "Man, let's hook up and get us a gig." So we got a five-piece band together and ended up at the Do-Dee

Club downtown on 9th and Hope streets. We were playing dance music. It was a non-union paying gig and we ended up staying at the Do-Dee for about six weeks. Shifty eventually became a respected bass player. He was also the composer of *Dark Shadows*, the song that Earl Coleman sang on Charlie Parker's third recording date for Dial Records, and *Jail House Rock*, which Elvis Presley recorded and made a mint on. But shifty didn't get a dime from Elvis for that song.

After the Do-Dee gig I got a job with Teddy Bunn's Spirits of Rhythm tiple group, playing swing, dance and cocktail music. I then had to join the Musician's Union Local 767. This was the black local, which was located at 16th and Central Avenue, near Washington Boulevard. With Teddy Bunn I played at Major Kaye's Supper Club on Cahuenga Boulevard in Hollywood, near Franklin. This turned into a good gig.

After working with Teddy Bunn I took Monk McFay's place on drums with Howard McGhee's band at the Down Beat Club at 42nd and Central Avenue. Howard had come out here with Coleman Hawkins and then just stayed on. Howard was playing bebop, *hard* bop, and that was exactly where I wanted to be. There were no bands here in Los Angeles who were playing the new thing, so I jumped at the opportunity to play with one of the great trumpet players of the times.

I had first caught Howard McGhee live in May of 1943. Along with J. D. King, the tenor saxophonist, he was playing in Andy Kirk's band. They were playing a dance at a ballroom in Washington DC, when I was playing the Howard Theater with Milton Larkin. I didn't get a chance to meet Howard then. Actually, it wasn't until I first heard *McGhee Special* that I truly became a big fan of his. He had joined Charlie Barnet's band and become famous. It wasn't until Howard came to Los Angeles in 1945 with Coleman Hawkins, stayed, organized his band and hired me that I actually met him. Maggie, as he was called by people who love him, was truly the "Bearer of Gifts," being the one who brought bebop to the West Coast as far as that's concerned.

He wanted his band to have its own sound. He got it. He wanted a semi-show band. He got it. He wanted a romping rhythm section. He got that too.

At that time the battles between two tenor saxophonists were becoming popular, à la Gene Ammons and Dexter Gordon's *Blowin' the Blues Away* with Billy Eckstine's big band. So Howard took Teddy Edwards off alto sax and put him on tenor, hired J. D. King and had the battle of the tenor saxes putting on a show. He later hired Tom Archia to replace J. D. King. Archia was a strong tenor man who'd also worked with me in Milton Larkin's big band.

Maggie was a beautiful person. He took care of business, had *class* and was intelligent. He was also a hell of a bandleader to work for. He was patient, understanding, and best of all was not on any ego trip. He taught me a lot. Maggie never got the recognition he deserved, but being a special person he lived with it. He was a great musician and trumpet player.

When I went to work for Maggie the drummers in Los Angeles were just playing swing drums, rudiments, para-diddling and ratamacuing. They just weren't happening. The drummers of note then were Lee Young (Lester's brother), Oscar Bradley, and Chico Hamilton. That was about it. I had been in New York the year before, in 1943, and was aware of what was happening musically all the way around, so I think I brought a little more to my playing than some of the others.

For his band Howard had hired Teddy Edwards out from under Roy Milton's blues band. Teddy had originally come with the Ernie Fields big band out of Oklahoma, but then decided to remain in Los Angeles when Fields moved on. Additionally, the band included Stanley Morgan on guitar, Vernon Biddle on piano, Robert "Dingbod" Kesterson on bass, J. D. King on tenor, and myself on drums. It was such a powerful group. The rest is history.

That band stayed busy. The Down Beat Club was our home base. We would go from there to Billy Berg's Swing Club on Hollywood Boulevard, then back to the Down Beat, then up to Hollywood again to the Streets of Paris on Hollywood Boulevard, the Jade Palace up the street, where we played opposite Kid Ory's dixieland band, back to the Down Beat, up to the Backstage Club in San Francisco, back to the Hi-De-Ho club at 50th and Western, with some one-nighters in San Diego along the way. I can't even remember all the places we played.

The band was getting all kinds of reviews from the so-called critics: good, bad, downright shitty. And these were from people that were not capable of understanding what we were doing musically. Yet they would be there all the time, listening. A lot of white musicians were there too, with mouth, nose, eyes and ears wide open in the process of what I call "Grand Theft of Musical Ideas." That's the way it was. I remember Norman Granz in the Streets of Paris with tennis shoes on, still a kid; Frankie Laine trying to sing with us at the Swing Club; Kay Starr on the same bill with us at the Streets of Paris, where we did live radio broadcasts; the Cats and a Fiddle group playing opposite us at the Streets. It goes on and on, but I can't recall everything.

When Dizzy Gillespie came out in 1945 to work Billy Berg's club, it had moved from Hollywood Boulevard and Las Palmas to Vine Street, right off Sunset. It was no longer called the Swing Club then. We were at the Streets of Paris when Charlie Parker just strolled in and came up on the stand. (Charlie was in town with Diz.) That was the first time I met Bird.

The Streets of Paris was situated downstairs off the street. When you walked in you came down off the sidewalk and the bandstand was above the bar, so you played down to the audience. The people there were spellbound when Bird got through playing. They had never heard anything like that in their lives. I knew I hadn't! I had heard Charlie Parker before on various records, but to be on the same stand and playing with him was a gas.

Howard McGhee's band had cut some sides for the Bihari brothers' record company, Modern, in 1945 and 1946. And so when Charlie Parker did his first session for Ross Russell's

Dial label in 1946 I was on them. Bird had talked to me the night I met him at the Streets of Paris. Where was I from? How old was I? How long had I been playing? He asked me all kinds of questions. He also said that he liked the way I played and that the only other dude from Colorado he knew was Paul Quinichette, the tenor saxophonist from Denver. He remarked that Colorado hadn't produced that many musicians whom he knew of.

Dizzy Gillespie had Charlie Parker, Ray Brown, Milt Jackson, Al Haig and Stan Levey in his group at Billy Berg's. When he closed there, Bird, Milt Jackson and Ray Brown stayed behind in Los Angeles. Bird started working with us when Howard could afford that many men on the stand or when the job called for a larger ensemble.

At that time Bird was in real bad shape due to his narcotic problem, so I will tell the world that Howard McGhee helped to keep Charlie Parker alive while he was so strung out in Los Angeles. In fact, Howard did more for Bird than anyone. Norman Granz had hired Bird for his Jazz at the Philharmonic concerts, but Bird fucked that up because he couldn't help himself.

Anyway, on 28 March 1946 we went into Radio Recorders recording studio on Santa Monica Boulevard in Hollywood around 10.00 a.m. and recorded *Moose the Mooche*, *Yardbird Suite*, *Ornithology* and *Night in Tunisia* in four hours, as the Charlie Parker Septet. In those days four sides were considered a session. These were all 78s. Anything over four hours was considered overtime, and since record companies were such cheap assholes anyway (still are when it comes to jazz), most sessions rarely went past four hours. So we worked slightly less than four hours.

On the way to the recording date, while I was driving him to the studio, Bird said that he had to finish a tune for the session. He was writing *Moose the Mooche* in the car from 35th and Maple streets on the east side of Los Angeles to Santa Monica Boulevard in Hollywood. He was a true genius.

Everyone remembers that famous four-bar break on *Night in Tunisia*, so I will tell the way that really went down.

Roy's parents, Charlotte and William Nelson Porter

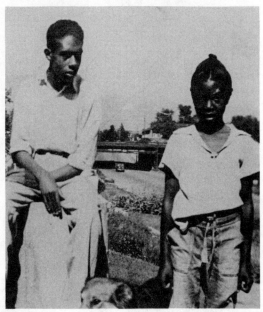

Roy aged about nine months　　　*Roy with his sister Evelyn, Colorado Springs, 1938*

The Milton Larkin Orchestra, Harlem Grill, Houston, 1937–8: (left to right) Henry Salone, William Luper (trombones); Lonnie Moore or Lester Patterson, Clifford Mitchell, Calvin Ladner (trumpets); Charles Gordon (drums); Lawrence Cato (bass); Arnett Cobb, Freddie Simon, Frank Domongeaux, Eddie "Cleanhead" Vinson (saxophones); George Lane (vocals) Milton Larkin (leader)

Aaron "T-bone" Walker, Club Rhumboogie, Chicago, 1943

Roy during his sophomore year at Wiley College, 1942–3

Mary Lincoln and Roy, San Francisco, 1946

Roy as a member of Howard McGhee's sextet, Billy Berg's Swing Club, Hollywood, 1945

Howard McGhee's sextet, Billy Berg's Swing Club, 1945 (left to right): Howard McGhee, Vernon Biddle, J.D. King, Bob "Dingbod" Kesterson, Teddy Edwards, Roy

Signed photograph of Charlie Parker with Mel Broiles, 1946

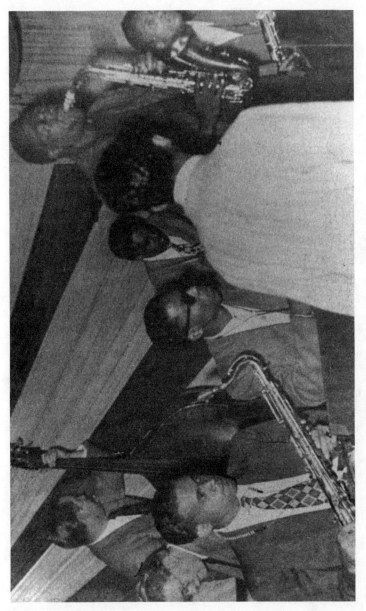

Howard McGhee's band, Club Finale, Los Angeles, 1946 (left to right): Earl Eklin, Bob "Dingbod" Kesterson, Gene Montgomery, Sonny Criss, Roy, Howard McGhee, Charlie Parker, Teddy Edwards

At the Club Finale, 1947 (left to right): Howard McGhee, Bill Jones, Earl Eklin, Sonny Criss, Charlie Parker, Bob "Dingbod" Kesterson, Teddy Edwards, Roy

Jam sessions at the Last Word Club on Central Avenue, 1946–7 (above, left to right): Kenny Bright, Barney Kessel, unknown, Maurice Simon, Teddy Edwards; (below) Sonny Criss, Clarence Jones, Wardell Gray, Kenny Bright

Eddie Davis's sextet at the 409 Club, San Pedro, c1946 (left to right): Robert Farlice, Leon Moore, Eddie Davis, William Lundy, Shifty Henry, Alice Young

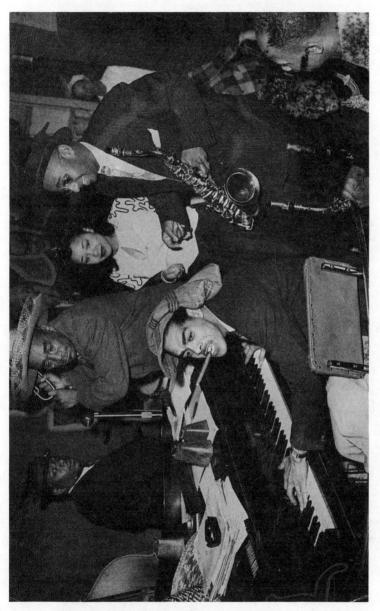

Jack McVea's band, 1947 (left to right): Rabon Tarrant, Sammy Yates, Thomas Crow, Mary Lincoln Porter, Jack McVea

Roy Porter's big band at the Club Alabam, Los Angeles, 1948 (left to right): Joe Harrison (piano); Alvy Kidd (congas); Joe Stone (bass); Roy (drums); Benny White (guitar); Robert Ross, Tony Anthony, Art Farmer (trumpets); Danny Horton, William Wiginton (trombones); Clifford Solomon, Leroy "Sweet Pea" Robinson, Eric Dolphy, Joe Howard, Clyde Dunn (saxophones)

Art Farmer during the recording session for Savoy, 1949

Roy as leader of the big band, Club Alabam, 1948

Leroy "Sweet Pea" Robinson and Eric Dolphy recording for Savoy, 1949

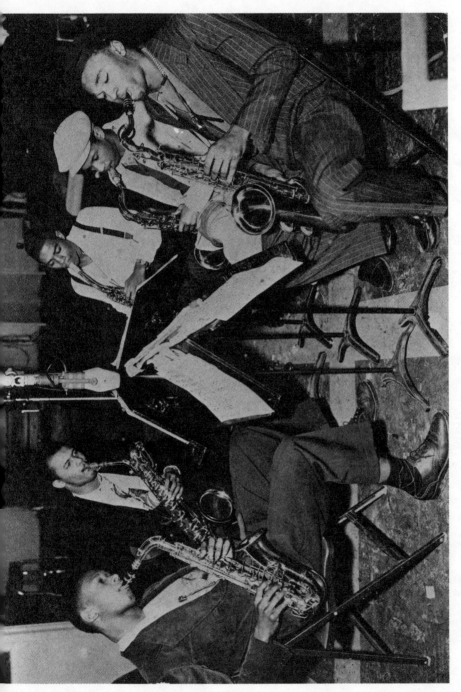

The saxophone section at the Savoy session, 1949 (left to right): Leroy "Sweet Pea" Robinson, Clyde Dunn, Eric Dolphy, Clifford Soloman, Joe Howard

Couldn't anyone count the break because Bird was doubling, tripling, quadrupling and everything else on what he played in those four bars. It was throwing all of us! Finally, Miles Davis said he would go in the corner and listen and bring his hand down on the first beat of the fifth bar. That's how the rhythm section came in right on time. I thought I'd set the record straight on that little bit of musical history. I know Miles has probably forgotten that.

In the meantime Central Avenue and the East Side were like the World's Fair, with people everywhere on the scene. Howard McGhee enlarged his band for a date at the Club Finale. The Finale was an after-hours place on First and San Pedro streets, located right downtown. The band included Howard on trumpet, Charlie Parker and Sonny Criss on alto saxophones, Teddy Edwards and Gene Montgomery on tenors, Earl Eklin on piano, Bob "Dingbod" Kesterson on bass and myself on drums. This band was really out of sight. (Dingbod was a real original and would strap his bass to the back of his little motor scooter and make all the jobs. I think he might even have driven to 'Frisco for the Backstage gig with his bass on his motor scooter.) But at the Finale Club we would keep audiences packed every morning until 6 a.m. Every musician, white or black, that came to Los Angeles to play places like The Orpheum or the Million Dollar Theater or any of the other clubs would swing by the Finale after hours digging what we were playing. Whenever they were in town most all of Stan Kenton's or Woody Herman's band were generally in there.

During this period, on 29 July 1946, Bird recorded his second session for Dial. This session was recorded at night and began around 11.00 p.m. We were off that night from the Hi-De-Ho. The recording took place at C. P. McGregor Studios on Western Avenue in Hollywood. In many ways it was a catastrophic date, but it turned out to be something of a classic also. I didn't think the results would ever be released, but they were. Charlie Parker couldn't finish the date and Howard McGhee had to play most of the melody by himself. Yard became quite ill during this record date because of his heroin problem. This eventually culminated in his spending time out at Camarillo State Hospital. Bird struggled through *Lover Man* and *The Gypsy*, but when he got to the songs *Bebop* and *Max Makin' Wax* he was totally out of it. He was a very sick man. But what he did play on those tunes was nothing but soul. Those sessions by the Charlie Parker Quintet are collectors' items today. The personnel on the date was Bird, Maggie, Jimmy Bunn on piano, Bob "Dingbod" Kesterson on bass and myself on drums.

The next night Bird was taken out of the Civic Hotel, where he was staying, down to the psychiatric ward at the County Jail because of a fire in his room. I wasn't there and I've heard so many conflicting stories concerning this episode that it is difficult to figure out what actually happened. It has also been said that he was found naked on top of a parked car on the street in front of the Civic. At any rate, they put him away for his behavior on this one. He did six months at Camarillo State Mental Hospital. After his release he recorded another date for Dial, where he sounds much stronger. From this came the great bop classic *Relaxin' at Camarillo*. After all of this Bird couldn't stay in Los Angeles, and not long after this last session for Ross Russell he split for New York.

I first heard Charlie Parker during my freshman year at Wiley College. Me and Wild Bill Davis, the organist, pianist, and arranger for the Wiley Collegians, were in a coffee shop just off campus eating, and suddenly we heard Jay McShann's big band playing *Confessin' the Blues* and *Hootie Blues* on the jukebox. I asked Wild Bill who the hell that was on alto and he replied, "Some bad cat from Kansas City." Charlie Parker was sounding so different and so *strong* that no one could really understand it, but we musicians recognized that he was something great.

I first met Bird's mentor when the Wiley Collegians were playing a weekend dance at the Regal nightclub in Dallas, Texas, on Thomas and Hall streets. His name was Buster Smith and he could really play the hell out of the alto saxophone. Buster told me that Bird had picked up a lot of his technique from him, and when I heard Buster play I damn sure believed him.

It is hard to talk about Yard, because I loved him so much. So did just about everyone he met. Charlie Parker was an extremely complicated individual. He sometimes acted like an innocent. He was not. Compassionate? He was. Thoughtful? He was not. Greedy? He was. Considerate? He was not. Demanding? He was. Envious? He was not. Outspoken? No. Mooche? He was, but he didn't have to be, because he was an idol to thousands of musicians and fans, young and old, that gave him anything he asked for. He could get money, food, sex, clothes, dope, transportation, instruments and anything else he wanted. That is the way Charlie Parker lived, *on other people*. They put him on a pedestal.

When I worked and recorded with Bird I lived at the Silverthorn Apartments on Maple and 35th streets. This was in 1946. Mrs Newman, my landlady, had rented a room to Bird at another house which she owned, over on Ascot Street. His room caught on fire from his smoking and Bird was evicted. So, I let him stay with me. One morning Mrs Newman came to collect her rent and caught Bird there. She said, "Both of you motherfuckers get out of my building." I had to move, but, sheeit, Bird felt nothing.

Everyone who had dealings with Charlie Parker came up on the short end. But most everyone still loved him because he truly didn't mean anyone any harm. He just couldn't help himself. He was an amazing person. I've seen him shoot smack, drop pills, smoke pot, drink booze and then get up on the stand and play the hell out of his horn.

I have performed with Bird at his best and at his worst. I remember nights at the Hi-De-Ho Club at 50th and Western Avenue when Bird was too loaded to play his horn and Maggie made him leave the bandstand. I also remember the nights when a young Hampton Hawes couldn't play the correct changes to certain tunes. Bird kept right on playing, not even letting you know you were wrong so you wouldn't feel bad on the bandstand. That happened to me also one night at the Suzi-Q club on Hollywood Boulevard. This was a one-nighter gig on our off-night from the Hi-De-Ho, but it was Bird's gig. Hampton Hawes, myself and Harry Babasin on bass were the rhythm section. We played *Koko*, which is actually Bird's treatment of *Cherokee*. I knew that I didn't play it right and I acknowledged this. Yard said, "That's alright man, you'll get it next time. Lend me a bean [dollar], will you?" What could I say or do? He was beautiful. Yet, for all of his ways, I never heard Charlie Parker put down another person.

It was always a mystery to me why Bird never talked about his childhood, but then Charlie Parker didn't talk much anyway. As they say, his horn did all the talking. The tragedy of his early death can be attributed to many, many things too numerous and complicated to even consider. But I do believe Bird died mostly of a broken heart, since he was never really accepted as the genius that he was. He made a lot of people quite wealthy, such as Herman Lubinsky, the owner of Savoy Records. And if Charlie Parker had not been black, he would have died a millionaire.

I hope that what I have said about Bird is not misconstrued to be a put-down. I loved Charlie Parker and always will. Millions of people all over the world do. But there is always something left to be desired in all human beings.

Los Angeles had a jumping jazz scene during those years. There were all sorts of joints that had good music, starting downtown at the Morris Hotel on Fifth Street. On Central Avenue at Washington Boulevard the Clark Hotel had a small bar that featured jazz music. Up at 22nd there was the Lincoln Theater. Across the street was the Jungle Room, down the way on 33rd was Jack's Basket Room. At Santa Barbara was the Elks Auditorium. Then, a little further south at 42nd was the Down Beat Club and directly across the street was the Last Word. A few doors down was the Club Alabam and the Dunbar Hotel, where all of the heavies of the black entertainment world stayed when they came through town. The Dunbar Grill in the hotel always had a lot of great music happening. In the next block was the Memo Club at 43rd, where Lorenzo Flennoy's trio played regularly.

Duke Ellington's singer Ivy Anderson had her place, Ivy's Chicken Shack, at Vernon and Central, while across the street Alex Lovejoy had an after-hours club upstairs. On Vernon just off Central was another nice room, the Ritz Club, where I had first met Teddy Bunn and the piano player Jack La Rue.

Central Avenue was a bitch all the way out to Watts, where the Plantation Club was located on 108th. Man, I can't even remember them all. Over on San Pedro Street near Adams Boulevard was a crazy after-hours spot named Cafe Society where Big Jim Wynn's Blues Band was the house band. Down the street at 28th was the Casablanca, another after-hours club. At 46th and Avalon was Herb Jeffries' Flamingo Club. Down farther was the Crystal Tea Room on 50th and Avalon, where the young sax men Walter Benton and Frank Morgan were first heard. At 53rd and Avalon was the Avalon Theater, which always had great shows. At South Park, located at 51st and Avalon, there were usually jazz concerts on Sunday afternoons sponsored by the City Parks and Recreation Department. Hell, LA was cooking and I haven't even scratched the surface. Clubs were springing up on the west side of LA like wildfire. During that time the west side was Vermont Avenue to Western, and there really were very few black people living in this area. Where the Crenshaw Center is now was wilderness.

There would be so many people on Central Avenue then between 42nd and Vernon that you couldn't walk without bumping into other folks. You'd see all sorts: soldiers, pimps, gangsters, hustlers, whores, movie stars, musicians, politicians, groupies, fans and, of course, the cops.

I can't overlook the California Club on Santa Barbara, off Western Avenue, where I played many times. A few years later Max Roach and Clifford Brown made some great music there. At Western near Florence there was the York Club, where trombonist Happy Johnson had a swinging little band which included Hampton Hawes on piano. Another joint was Strip City. This was a swinging club with jazz music and strippers. Located at Western and Pico, it was where I first heard (somewhat later) Ramsey Lewis and his trio of Holt and Young on drums and bass. These days there's the Tiki Club on Western near Exposition, but it used to be the old Waikiki Club in the early 1940s on through the 1950s and 1960s. It was called Mike's Waikiki Club, but Mike was a diehard racist who would not admit black people. His club was decorated with coconuts and palm trees inside. He had a Hawaiian bell hung up over the bar so he could ring it for every drink sold. Finally he gave the club up and it became the Tiki Club. Mike was a tragic figure but funny.

The jam sessions were legendary and were all over LA at all times. You could leave the Down Beat or Club Alabam and go to Jack's Basket Room and maybe the Casablanca, then end up at the Flamingo for a blowing session, all in one night. At these jam sessions, especially at the Down Beat and Jack's Basket Room, musicians would be playing their asses off, musicians like Dexter Gordon, Wardell Gray, Teddy Edwards, Howard McGhee, Miles Davis, Al Killian, Oscar Pettiford, Barney Kessel, Hampton Hawes, the guitarist Big Tiny Webb, Benny Bailey, Sonny Criss, Chuck Thompson, Lucky Thompson, Charles Mingus, Shifty Henry, Charlie Parker, Earl Coleman the singer and Clarence Jones. Jones was the premier bebop jazz player in LA at that time; he died later tragically from a heroin overdose. This list really only scratches the surface. There were a great number of younger musicians who later became famous who were just hanging out then too, such as Clora Bryant, Lavonne Tyus, Vi Redd, Horace Tapscott and Lawrence Marable, among so many others.

Since World War II was still raging on at this point, there was a "brownout" on throughout the city. Residents were told to keep all of their shades down during this time because of the fear of Japanese bomb attacks. This also meant that the street and commercial lights all had to go out at 12 midnight. And since the clubs had to close at 12 p.m., you also had to start your gig early at 7 p.m. All of this, however, made for a special feeling and fostered a certain sense of comaraderie too.

About this time I came up with the idea to bend the top of a metal music stand so it could be used as a floor cymbal stand in order to get the type of sound that I wanted. This let me have my ride cymbals slanted at an angle so I could hit them in the middle and get a nice, sharp, clean sound. Up until then, all drummers' cymbals that I had seen were sitting flat, straight across like pie plates. Later the Slingerland Drum Company started manufacturing holders that allowed drummers to regulate cymbals at any angle. That idea came from me, but at the time I didn't have the perspicacity to realize what this innovation might mean for the drum world. The next thing I knew, all of the modern drummers were playing cymbals at an angle, and to this day they don't even know where the idea came from. I have never received credit or monies from drum or cymbal companies, or acknowledgement and recognition from the drum community for my innovation.

As far as jam sessions go one of the greatest of all time that was actually recorded took place at the Elks Auditorium in Los Angeles on 6 July 1947. *Jeronimo,* which is the tune *Cherokee,* was played for almost an hour, and was released originally on the old Bop Records label. It was later reissued by Savoy on an LP called *The Hunt,* and features Dexter Gordon and Wardell Gray along with Trummy Young, Howard McGhee, Red Callender, Barney Kessel, Sonny Criss, Hampton Hawes, Teddy Edwards and myself. That Sunday afternoon the Elks Auditorium was packed to capacity and the music was truly memorable!

By this point the bebop scene had caught on. More clubs were giving the music a chance, which allowed some of us musicians to make some change even if only for a one-night session. The Zanzibar Club on Vernon and San Pedro streets began booking modern music, and Dex, Hampton Hawes, Art Farmer and I gigged there for a while. Soon the Cricket Club on Washington Boulevard just off Vermont hired Diz's big band for a week's engagement. Horace Henderson and Vernon "Geechie" Smith's orchestras were the house bands there for quite a while.

The Cricket Club was another story in itself. Before I left for New York with Dexter Gordon in January of 1948, Paul and Harry Rubin, the club's owners, hired Geechie Smith as the house band. This was late 1947. Smith became manager and entertainment director. Prior to this, Blacks were not welcome. Smith was responsible for integrating the club. He hired Dizzy, and during Diz's two week stint all of the Hollywood movie stars like Ava Gardner, who liked the new thing in music, regularly came by. When I came back to LA from back east in June of 1948, I stopped in for a jam session on a Sunday afternoon and the place was jumping.

I am not comfortable throwing names around, but I must mention one of the finest musicians in Los Angeles who never got the recognition that he deserved. Eddie Davis, not Lockjaw, was a solid tenor sax man and one hell of an arranger. During the Central Avenue boom he had the only other band that was anywhere near Howard McGhee's band as far as charts were concerned. He wasn't quite at Howard's level because he didn't have the same caliber of musicians, but it was still a monster group. Eddie was pretty sharp and worked continually at the Twin Bells Club on Slauson Avenue off Central. Additionally, he had San Pedro, the city near Long Beach, all locked up. In that town he played at the 409 Club, the Senate Club, and the Shanghai, which were all located in the waterfront section.

Back in downtown LA, Gerald Wilson's big band could be heard frequently down at Shep's Playhouse near First and San Pedro streets. Eddie Heywood had the gig downstairs in the lounge at Shep's. This club didn't last too long though, and was closed due to fraud.

Shep's, the Club Finale, and the Civic Hotel were all situated in an area of downtown Los Angeles which had been Little Tokyo before World War II: most all of the businesses there belonged to Japanese Americans. When the US declared war on Japan after Pearl Harbor all Japanese Americans were sent to concentration camps and their businesses were confiscated. A lot of black people took over some of these places and the district became more integrated. Places like the Civic Hotel, which previously had a different name and where Blacks couldn't even get a room, became integrated. Years later, after the war ended, the Japanese Americans were able to get their businesses back. But during that time this Little Tokyo area became something of a Mecca for black music and was really swinging. Eventually, as is usually the case in Los Angeles, the old buildings were torn down for "civic development" and this area lost a lot of its character.

Billy Eckstine, the gifted singer who had such a popular following at this time, played Los Angeles with his big band at the Plantation Club. The second time in 1947 he was at the Club Alabam. There, Lana Turner was on the scene a lot, because she had eyes for Mr B.

It was while Mr B's big band was out here in 1947 that me and Art Blakey got tight. I heard that band and said to myself that if I ever got a big band together it would have that feeling. Art Blakey was really kicking Mr B's big band like a drummer should! The band members were staying at the Morris Hotel downtown on 5th Street. So one day I went down to meet Art. He told me how good I sounded on the Dial record session with Bird, which was a surprise to me. I told him I didn't know the difference between a paradiddle and a five-stroke roll. He burst out laughing and couldn't believe it. Then he proceeded to show me how to play a paradiddle, saying, "You've been doing this all the time, but just didn't know it." He also showed me how to practice with over-sized sticks on a pillow so they wouldn't bounce back. This is a great practice method, since you will have more power when you're playing your drums. Art Blakey is one of the greatest, most powerful drummers in the world. In addition, he happens to be one of the most beautiful people in the world. He is the only drummer that ever took the time to show me anything relating to drumming technique.

At the Club Alabam during these same days Cecil "Big Jay" McNeely first started making a name for himself. McNeely was originally a jazz player to be reckoned with until he found a gimmick and started making money by walking the bar and marching out into the street while still playing the horn.

The first black DJs in Los Angeles were Joe Adams on KOWL, Roy Loggins at KALI, and Bill Sampson on KWKW, who broadcast live from Jack's Basket Room. Charles Trammell of KGFJ was another jock who did live broadcasts. His were from the window of Dolphin's of Hollywood record store on Vernon and Central. He was a rhythm-and-blues man but he'd play jazz records also and was a very hip dude.

Meanwhile, back at the ranch, Howard's band was at the Streets of Paris and we were burning. One night I'm playing my ass off and all of a sudden a whiskey shot glass whizzes by my head. It scared the shit out of me because I didn't see this cracker when he threw it at me, since a white broad was smiling and making eyes at me. That jerk was ejected from the club that night but was right back there the next evening. If that glass had hit me I'd probably be dead.

In the clubs socializing between the races was cool, but if the LAPD goon squad saw you with a white chick on the streets or in an automobile that was another story. The first thing you'd see was flashing red lights pulling you over. One cop then would talk to the chick on the passenger side of the car while the other cop would talk to you like you had a tail. Invariably the cops would ask the chick what she was doing with a nigger and call her a nigger lover. Sometimes they'd make the women get in the police car and then they'd drive them back to Hollywood or wherever they were from. The next night at the club the broads would run everything down to me. Those cops were ignorant and really up tight. I've read in Hampton Hawes's book *Raise Up Off Me* about how many flashing red lights were evident on Central Avenue in the 1940s. Supposedly they were looking for knives and guns. Bullshit: they were there to harass black musicians and the black pimps that had white whores or any black men with white women.

Some of these white women were nice ladies, while others were groupies, chippies, bitches and whores. But they were all beautiful people who liked the revolutionary bebop music that we were playing. They were all good to me – mentally, physically, spiritually and most of all *financially*. Miles Davis had a chick then that had big eyes for him and wanted to help him financially to the tune of about 200 dollars. Miles didn't know quite whether to take it or not. I told him if he didn't accept that money that I would kick his ass myself, because he damned sure needed it. And Miles took the bread.

The heat really didn't have to worry about how many guns or knives were around because there were plenty of Uncle Tom snitches who kept the police informed of anything and everything that went down in the neighborhood. But what these red-neck cops didn't realize was that the bebop and jazz that the black musicians were playing was bringing the races closer together. This music was new and the majority of the listeners didn't really understand it, but they *wanted* to be enlightened. Seems like it's always been the case anyway that the most intelligent peoples are the ones that dig jazz. But the cops came up against something new when they encountered a lot of the bebop musicians. They had no idea that they weren't dealing with ignorant Uncle Tomming black nigger musicians.

Bebop turned that shit around. Bebop also became quite popular, and, just as with a lot of black culture and music, it was soon widely imitated and eventually stolen – a catastrophe of enormous proportions.

Back in the clubs during 1944, my first experience working with Benny Carter was at a club named Diane's on 8th or 9th Street near Alvarado in the Westlake District. It was interesting because the club was supposedly owned by Buggsy Siegel and was operated by the notorious Virginia Hill, his woman. Our band there at Diane's, if my memory serves me correctly, consisted of Benny; Bumps Meyers, tenor sax; Charlie Drayton, bass; Gerald Wiggins, piano; and myself on drums.

Over the years many people have asked me why this music was called bebop, which is a good question. I'm no authority on that but I'm sure that the phrase was coined by someone who was not a musician. I can say that the lines and solos of many tunes were played in such a way that the phrasing of the notes sounded like you were saying the word bebop. Scat singing helped popularize the term. Diz, who isn't a bad scat singer, may have had a hand in that. Of course, he also wrote the tune *Bebop*, which became popular, and which I recorded later with Charlie Parker. Other great scat masters include Babs Gonzales, Kenny "Pancho" Hagood and Joe Carroll. The latter two were both singers in Diz's bands. Ella Fitzgerald really made this type of music famous for female singers, and Sarah Vaughan, Betty "Be Bop" Carter (as she used to be known) and Carmen McRae all sing bebop. Jon Hendricks is a master at it.

One of the publications that helped promote and keep this music alive was the *California Eagle*. This was the first black newspaper in Los Angeles, to my knowledge. The *Eagle* had a more positive approach and attitude toward the jazz movement at that time because of journalists like the late J. T. Gipson, the first husband of the writer Gertrude Gipson. J. T. helped keep my band alive as well as the whole bebop movement in Los Angeles, where bop was initially neither appreciated nor understood. The other black newspaper, the *Los Angeles Sentinel*, came a few years later, and, unlike the *Eagle*, their attitude was definitely not as positive towards jazz.

I decided I needed a change from California and in January 1948 I left Los Angeles with Dexter Gordon. Our first gig was at the Pershing Lounge in Chicago. That band included Tadd Dameron on piano. He was a big influence on my career as a composer and arranger and was also such a fine piano player. The others were Kenny Dorham on trumpet, Curly Russell on bass and Earl Coleman on vocals.

In Chicago I happened to cross paths with a kid drummer who lived there named Ike Day. Considering that we didn't actually stay too long in Chicago, I got to know Ike quite well. Ike would come to your gig while you were setting up and say, "Hey, man, I play a little drums. Do you need any help? Can I tune your tom toms for you?" That's how he got to be known as one of the baddest drummers in the world. He would start playing on your drums and you wouldn't want him to stop because he had his own original thing going. He did Art Blakey, Max Roach, me and all the others like that. I loved the dude. Sad to say, he couldn't get many gigs because even at that early age he was strung out on smack, and he died a few years later. But Ike Day was a *monster* on drums. Music lost a very talented drummer when he passed. Plus, he was so young. Meeting him was one of the best experiences I have ever had.

After the Pershing Lounge in Chicago, Dexter's group played the Hotel Du Sable Lounge and the Sunset Terrace Ballroom in Indianapolis on our way to the Three Deuces on 52nd Street in New York.

When we got to the Apple one of the worst blizzards in history hit our asses. Next, the Three Deuces gig didn't last but two weeks, and to top it all off Dex was having his Jones problems, so there was no money and things got really fucked up. This was the second time I'd been to New York and it felt quite different from 1943. In 1948 I had acquired a little bit of a name since I'd recorded those Dial sessions with Charlie Parker, but I still ended up stranded.

The thing that saved me was the fact that I knew a few people, like Art Blakey, the drummer Joe Harris, Kenny Dorham (who had been my roommate at Wiley College), Howard McGhee, Doc West and Earl Coleman. I would eat at either Art's, Kenny's, Maggie's (he'd just come back to New York from LA) or Doc West's. I had befriended Doc a few months earlier in Los Angeles when he was in town with Erroll Garner. Doc needed a cymbal for the recording session with Bird and Earl Coleman, so I loaned him the cymbal but it was never returned. I guess he figured he owed me. Diz's drummer, Teddy Stewart, helped me out too. I was also able to get a small loan from Gerald Wilson, who happened to be in New York with Basie's band. Gerald was staying at the Hotel Theresa. Blacks were finally allowed to live there. I'll never forget Joe Medlin, the singer, who also helped me out

(I saw Joe in LA in 1973 when he was an A & R man for Polydor Records, and I got a chance to thank him again). I didn't see much of Max because he didn't live in Harlem where I was hanging out. Minton's was *the* place where everything was happening, since most of the clubs on 52nd Street were closing. Shortly after I left I know the Deuces became a strip joint.

Finally, a bandleader named Candy Carter came to my rescue. Carter got my car out of hock and I went out with him and his rhythm-and-blues band on some one-nighters down into Virginia. We played Richmond, Portsmouth, Norfolk and a lot of places not even on the map. But it was fine with me because I was able to get back on my feet. After returning to New York I played a gig with Howard McGhee, but I can't even remember where. I saw Bird. He was into the same old shit, and asked me to drive him somewhere to score and so I did. A West Indian woman had set my drums and clothes out into the hall because I owed her ten dollars for back rent. Luckily, her young son liked bebop music and me too, so he called a cab and took me to one of his girlfriends' apartment. I was able to stay there until I moved into a building owned by Lionel and Gladys Hampton at 48 St Nicholas Place. I don't recall that youngster's name, but I have never forgotten that act of kindness.

In New York during this same period there was a very important black man called Father Divine. He had a congregation of followers, both black and white, throughout the country who believed that he was God. His disciples sent money and gifts to his organization or cult and he became a millionaire. Of course, he was a con man in much the same manner as Jim Jones, the Bagwan Ragneesh and Reverend Moon, but Father Divine did do something to help out the poor people of this country. Father Divine had restaurants in many of the large cities of the country where the poor could get a meal for no more than 25 cents. There were others involved in similar hustles, such as a homosexual from Detroit called Prophet Jones and another character who called himself Daddy Grace in Los Angeles, but Father

Divine had the most followers then in the later 1940s and was the most famous. Being stranded in New York then, it was a big help to be able to eat so cheaply at Father Divine's restaurants, and these little eateries helped me out of some tough spots.

New York in 1948 was starting to change as more and more musicians became strung out on heroin. Luckily, I didn't get strung at that point. I was able to get by with the help of some old friends and some very kind new ones, all of whom helped me out tremendously.

While knocking around in the Apple, I came to the conclusion that this city was more of a dog-eat-dog existence than anywhere I had ever been before. People were just too cold. If you happened to be in someone's apartment around meal time they would sneak off and eat. One person would sit and bullshit you in the living room while the other went into the kitchen to eat. When that "friend" got through eating, he'd come back and keep you company while the other dude would go eat, never even thinking of inviting you to share some of the beans and rice they were having. I told myself, "Fuck this shit, I'm not used to this jive."

I'd caught a foxy little chick named Rose in 1943 that lived across the street from the Braddock Hotel on 126th Street. When she found out that I was back in town she looked me up. I said, "Sheeit. This is nice!" I was convinced that she had forgotten all about me. Thanks too to her help I was able to survive, God bless her.

Art Tatum's former guitar player Tiny Grimes called me up one day for a gig. The job was in Cleveland, Ohio. I left New York, glad to be getting out of town. Cleveland turned out to be a swinging city, which I enjoyed much better than New York. It was not as frantic as the Apple, was much more laid back and the people were just more down to earth. Additionally, you talk about some fine, big-legged, sexy broads – Cleveland would "shock you in your socket" for all of the women there. We had a great gig there at a place called the Tijuana Club. This was one of the finest clubs I had ever played in. The club had a revolving bandstand over the bar and it had mirrors all around covering the entire room, so any way you looked you'd generally see something pretty.

Tiny Grimes was beautiful to work with. He was a real gentleman, in addition to being able to play his ass off without using a guitar pick. The only dude that I thought was an asshole was Red Prysock on tenor saxophone. This "wham-de-bam" jerk would bug me to play a loud back-beat on everything. I told him to kiss my ass and the battles were on every night. I'd already been approached by Lionel Hampton to join his band, but all his drummers had to continually play that pounding back-beat, so I declined going out on the road with Gates. If I didn't do it for Lionel Hampton, I damned sure wasn't going to hear that shit from some sideman.

I got tired of this nonsense and so finally I told Tiny I'd stay on until he got someone else to play drums. About this time I also got in touch with Mary (also known as Judy) in Los Angeles, and heard that she had a new Cadillac waiting for me there. So I just split. I'd also made up my mind that I was going to get my own band together when I got out to LA. I had felt for some time that I had to put something together on my own, because truthfully I was really tired of being a "follower" in other people's bands and wanted to be out on my own leading my own band.

In Cleveland, a dude called Count DuBarry, who played some piano and who'd been in Candy Carter's band with me in New York, was traveling with me. The Count had wanted to leave New York and so we were sharing the driving along the way. He'd also help me to set up my drums. So when Tiny Grimes found my replacement, we said our goodbyes and started on that long drive west. The trip back was beautiful. When we were driving through San Bernardino on Route 66 the California weather was spectacularly inspiring. When we hit Los Angeles I knew that I was back on my own turf.

5

Big Band

The first thing I started to do when I hit Los Angeles in 1948 was to get my own band together. My idea was to have either a quintet or sextet, or even a septet, but I wanted some of the younger musicians that were showing promise. I got on the phone and called Joe Stone, a bass player that I'd worked with before, along with Robert Ross, a trumpet man. Ross called the tenor saxophonist and arranger Joe Howard. I still had Count DuBarry with me and he played piano for a while. But he really couldn't cut our music and so I hired Joe Harrison as our pianist. We started rehearsing at the Chicken Shack on Vernon near Avalon Boulevard in June of 1948.

This little quintet began sounding pretty good and by and by musicians and other folks started hanging around the rehearsals at the Chicken Shack. One day a guy named Blondie Smith came in and asked me if I would be interested in enlarging the band to eight pieces in order to do some USO shows. I thought a moment and told him that this would be no problem. Good musicians were dropping by every day and there was always somebody who wanted to join the band. Next thing I knew, Clifford Solomon, Clyde Dunn and Wiggie Wiginton came on board and we had our octet. Blondie was a singer and he had brought a tune of his, *Love Is Laughing at Me,* along to our rehearsal. Joe Howard made an arrangement on it and we eventually recorded it.

After about two solid weeks of rehearsing, Blondie Smith's USO tour fell through, but I was determined to make it happen musically. I liked the sound we were getting, although the group at this point was not strictly a jazz group, since we were rehearsing for these USO shows that were going to be paying nice bread.

About this time Joe Howard said, "Man, I've got some charts for 17 pieces. How about it?" Robert Ross chimed in that he had some big-band charts also. And that was it. I looked up the next day and there must have been 20 guys there at rehearsal.

The Chicken Shack was right on an alley on Vernon, and on the way home from school the kids would stop off and buy chicken and take it home or eat it there. Business began booming there at the Shack. It had a little bandstand with a piano on the side of the room. Figuring I had nothing to lose, I asked the owner what he would charge to let me rehearse 17 pieces there. I also asked him if we could move the bandstand to the back of the room, since there just wasn't the room now. The owner told me that he wouldn't charge me anything as long as we rehearsed in the afternoon and early evenings, since this would be good for his business. He was quite a nice man and also said that he admired what I was trying to put together.

As soon as word got around that a big band was rehearsing, people started coming in off the streets in droves, especially the school kids. The music was sounding so good, and I asked myself, "Where did these bad young cats come from?" In truth I had never heard any of Joe Howard's or Robert Ross's arrangements before and was pleasantly surprised by both of their work. Joe also helped me round up the right musicians.

We had five saxes, four trumpets, three trombones and five rhythm players. Joe Howard next began pulling my coat about a good alto player to play first chair who was attending Los Angeles City College. Shortly thereafter, in walks this funny looking dude, looking like a junior high-school student, with an alto case in one hand and a flute or clarinet case in the other. He turned out to be Eric Dolphy. When I first met Eric he reminded me of a doctor or lawyer or even a Certified Public Accountant. He was very polite and had a nice personality. He was actually rather quiet at this time and seemed a bit shy, especially with the chicks.

At the other extreme was our valet, James Robinson. We

called him the Cisco Kid and drinking wine was his thing. He did a better job of keeping the band supplied with wine and pills than of doing his job as a valet. But he was with the band just because he loved me and everyone that was in the band. In fact Cisco actually worked for nothing but the love of the music and the fellows who were his family. He would set up the music stands, pack all the books of the arrangements, set up mikes and lights, pack and set up my drums and run all errands at rehearsal or on a gig. He was a beautiful person, just like a brother to me, and I don't know *anyone* that didn't love him. When I had the money I would rent a place for him and when we couldn't do that he would damn sure stay with me. I remember one gig when he was so loaded he packed everything up when it was over but he left all the band's arrangements on the bandstand and forgot about them. I didn't know about it until a few days later at rehearsal and everyone was ready to play and – no music. Luckily we were able to call the Zenda Ballroom, located at that time on 9th Street near Figueroa downtown, and the music was still there. I had to fire him for that, but it was only temporary, until the next gig. He would mess up all the time because he loved that vino, but Cisco was the only valet we ever had. If I talked about firing Cisco too much, the cats in the band probably would have kicked my ass.

With Eric riding hard as first alto, our reed section started to come together. In came Art Farmer and soon he had the brass section sounding just like clockwork. The next week Jimmy Knepper the trombonist asked if he could rehearse with the band. I wasn't that particular, frankly, about white boys being in the band because I wanted to keep a loose, swinging feeling. But when he played he sounded so good that I jokingly asked him if his mother or father were black. Knepper just laughed and kept on burning.

Meantime, word was getting out about the rehearsals at the Chicken Shack and it stayed packed with people. One evening a Mr Jackson, that owned an employment office on Central Avenue and 54th Street, came in. He explained that his daughter had told him good things about the band. He too liked the sounds, but wanted to know whether we had a manager and had some different jobs lined up. I told him that we really hadn't gotten that far yet. Being a business-man and a hustler, Mr Jackson asked us, if he put on a dance in Bakersfield for a weekend, would we consider going up there to play. We all talked it over and decided we had nothing to lose, so I told him that we were on. Jackson rented this ballroom on the main highway going into Bakersfield. He then hired a dude whom everyone knew as "Tack 'em up" to tack up placards on billboards, telephone poles, fences, storefronts and just about everywhere all over Bakersfield.

While this was going on, Joe Howard, Robert Ross and Jimmy Knepper were all bringing in arrangements at almost every rehearsal, so the book was sufficient to play a dance even if we had to repeat some tunes. Since this was our first gig we had to have some manner of uniforms, so we settled on dark blue suits. Our vocalist Paul Sparks talked his mother into making us some light blue fluff bow ties. But the ties were the only things that matched.

We didn't give a damn; we had a gig. Cisco had picked up our supply of bennies and wine, so we were cool. We took off north from Los Angeles in three cars and a pickup truck for the instruments.

Friday night about 25 or 30 people showed. But the band was sounding good. Saturday night maybe 100 folks came out, standing listening and dancing. By this point the band was cooking. Sunday night more than 200 people showed, but we didn't make more than a few dollars each for all of our efforts. Bakersfield was then as it is now: a white country-and-western town that really catered to that kind of music. The ballroom that we played was rented to us on the basis that we pay the rent for it out of the take at the door. Additionally, the door had to cover all of our expenses and salaries.

Our audience was mostly black and at that time Bakers-field had only a sparse black population. The section of town where these people lived was called Cottonwood Road. This stretch had barbecue joints, beer joints, other businesses and a small motel where we stayed. It was a real cut-throat environment, but it was that way because of the segregated nature of Bakersfield, just like the South. Cottonwood Road was one long, unpaved street where 90 per cent of Bakersfield's black inhabitants lived. When we came up there and played this dance it was something new and exciting for these people, because all that they were used to was rhythm-and-blues records from the jukeboxes in the beer joints. That ballroom dance was a catastrophe as far as any money made was concerned, but that gig made me think strongly about trying to keep the band together.

Back in Los Angeles we were still rehearsing at the Chicken Shack when Hunter Hancock, the famous white rhythm-and-blues DJ, walked in and liked what he heard. He booked the band into Billy Berg's club on Vine Street for a Sunday afternoon matinee and the place was packed. The bandstand was so small the rhythm section was on it and the rest of the band was on the floor. That gig made up my mind to keep the band together whatever. Hunter Hancock started having me as a guest quite often on his "Harlem Matinee" radio show on station KRKD on Western Avenue (the station later became KGFJ). That helped the band when we would have a gig at the Elks Auditorium, Avadon Ballroom or wherever. He was interested in the band and proved it by later playing the records I recorded.

By this time musicians, black, white, brown or whatever, knew when and where the band was rehearsing and would be there with their axes just in case any of the regular guys didn't show. Joe Howard was a young man with the uncanny ability to write an arrangement that had modern chord structural harmonies, not too complex, that would swing at all times. Robert Ross, I think, was a little more advanced in his writing, because he had more experience and was older. He had already done some charts for Gerald Wilson and Ray Charles's bands and was a good section man. Ross's arrangements were filled with intricate passages for each section to play. You really had to be thinking about what you were doing to play his arrangements. But they would swing like a pendulum if played right. Jimmy Knepper's charts were good, period. He had played in the old Boyd Raeburn band and it had been a good band. At first I didn't know why so many players wanted to be in my band, but then I realized it had to be the rapport we all had with each other; each player could experiment and play what he felt within the confines of any given chart. Most of all, at my rehearsals everyone had fun. The guys didn't treat me like I was a bandleader; it was just like one happy family. I know it was love and respect. Another thing is that most of the up-and-coming musicians were young and they were ripe for some fresh ideas, so my rehearsals were the place to be. There are only a few musicians of that day who didn't either rehearse or play – mostly rehearse – with that band at one time or another during the two years it was in existence.

The personnel of the band would change at almost every rehearsal, especially the reed section, due to a lot of things such as no money to catch the streetcar to get there, etc. If Eric couldn't make it, due to a lesson, Herb Geller would. If Sweetpea Robinson was absent, Joe Maini or Gene Gravens took over. If Hadley Caliman wasn't there, Clifford Solomon would be. Joe Howard was very seldom gone, but in his absence William "Boogie" Daniels or Wilbur Brown showed. I remember young Chet Baker, even before he started playing flugelhorn, would fill in at the Chicken Shack when another trumpet player didn't show for rehearsal. But all in all, the band was pretty stable under the circumstances.

I remember the first appearance we made where we had many replacements. It was a concert in 1948 in the auditorium at LA City College presented by Bob Fox and Dick Bock. They presented jazz artists regularly, but in the mornings around 10.30 a.m. Some of the guys were in school or day jobs. At the time Eric Dolphy and Vi Redd were classmates on the campus. No problem for Eric, he was right in the "kitchen." Fox and Bock were fellow students at LACC, interested in jazz. Dick Bock later formed World Pacific Jazz Records. He was the first to record *Lonesome*

Mood, with the Titans vocal group on his label in 1958, but failed to push the record.

The two mainstays of the trombone section were William "Wiggie" Wiginton and Jimmy Knepper. I always had a little trouble with 'bone players because good ones were in demand. The rhythm section mostly stayed the same because only three bass players were with the band off and on: Addison Farmer, Joe Stone and Roger Alderson. Paul Sparks became the main vocalist. Damita Jo, then just 16 or 17, sang with the band for about three months. Charles Rene, mainly our conga player, also sang. He later sang with Spade Cooley's country-and-western band. Art Farmer, Eddie Preston and Robert Ross were the mainstays of the trumpet section. Art was on first trumpet with Robert and Eddie on any part. Ross was also arranger, so it didn't make any difference who came in, it was cool. That band was an institution within itself. I would always keep a conga player that played drums as well, because I would play some boogie-woogie piano with arrangements behind me. I'd also stand up and bullshit in front of the band. It was a gas. Clyde Dunn was always on baritone saxophone from the beginning. Benny White was the only guitar player I ever used. Joe Harrison was the regular pianist.

I didn't start dropping "bennies" until I came to Los Angeles in 1944. By that time pot was passé for me because I had never liked the feeling it gave me anyway. Pot (marijuana) made me self-conscious and a bit paranoid. It afforded no relaxation at all, especially while playing my instrument. Pot was good to sit and dig sounds with. Benzedrine was sold in two forms, pills and the inhalers. It was legal to buy the inhalers over the counter, but you were supposed to have a prescription for the pills. The pills were used legally, mainly by airline pilots, bus drivers, etc. – anyone who had to stay alert and awake in their occupation. The inhaler was a different story; anyone could purchase them. The benzedrine was inside the inhaler, saturated in an orange-coloured paper strip. At that time we were drinking Molotov Cocktails, which is white port wine mixed with lemon juice. Man, we would get four or five quarts of white port, buy some inhalers, break them open, put the strips in each bottle of wine, put the wine next to a heater or heat, and let it sit and dissolve for a few days. When you drink that shit, man it will blow your mind, but we would be feeling mellow being loaded for days without any ZZZ's. Cisco knew exactly how long to let it set and dissolve, just like a moonshiner.

By this time we had started rehearsing at the Club Alabam on Central Avenue because the Chicken Shack was getting too crowded and there were too many distractions. I started having closed rehearsals and we began taking care of business.

Ralph Bass, an A & R man from Savoy Records, called me from New York and said he would be in town and wanted to come by rehearsal and hear the band. I gave him the go-ahead and he flew out from New York. He came to our rehearsal and after we finished playing we signed a contract to cut four sides. In those days all records were 78s. On 29 January 1949 we went into Radio Recorders recording studio on Santa Monica Boulevard in Hollywood and cut *Sippin' with Cisco, Gassin' the Wig, This is You* and *Pete's Beat*. During this time period recordings were made disc to disc in mono; there was no stereo. We had only one mike for five saxes, another mike for the seven brass instruments, and one more for the five rhythm players.

The owner of Savoy Records, Herman Lubinsky, was called Herman "the Vermin" by many of his colleagues in the record industry. I know in his dealings with me I foolishly gave up the rights to my material, so in a sense he beat me out of that, just as he did Charlie Parker and many others who recorded for him.

I had no knowledge that the big band's songs had even been released until someone told me that they had heard the records on a jukebox somewhere in Texas. Then on 23 February 1949 Lubinsky flew out personally for the second session. We went into the studio and recorded *Little Wig, Phantom Moon, Howard's Idea* and *Love is Laughing at Me*. Titles we recorded at another session, including *A Sunday Kind of Love*, featuring a fine trumpet solo by James Metlock, have never been released. Savoy was heavily into jazz previously, but they had just recorded a tenor saxophonist named Paul Williams and had a million-seller called *The Hucklebuck*. So my recordings were a case of the right place at the wrong time. Roy Porter and his 17 Beboppers was put on the shelf for 29 years. Incidentally, Savoy hung that name on the band. I just called it the Roy Porter 17-piece Big Band. But when *Little Wig* and *Gassin' the Wig* were released as 78s, the name printed on the label was Roy Porter and his 17-piece Beboppers, and the name stuck.

Out of all of this the band became a little better known and started rehearsing and working more. The musicians I had in that band just loved to play those charts and were very giving of their time. So, we began to play such venues as the Avadon Ballroom, the Zenda Ballroom, Lincoln Theater, Avalon Theater, Club Alabam, Jack's Basket Room, the Jungle Room, the Elks Hall, San Pedro Club, the Hole in the Wall and just about anywhere else we could during this period of 1948 through 1949 and on into 1950.

We also played quite a few club dances. These were affairs put on by women and their sororities. Frequently these involved fashion shows also, and took place at the Zenda Ballroom in downtown Los Angeles. As far as the other places which I've mentioned go, the Lincoln Theater presented stage shows weekly and at Christmas hosts of bands and entertainers performed there free all day. Admission to the public was Christmas baskets or toys for the poor. The Avalon Theater presented stage shows periodically also. The Club Alabam was probably the most famous club in town in the late 1940s. It featured name bands and shows with chorus girls, plus dancing six nights a week. The Jungle Room was a little place that was both a before- and after-hours club. Jack's Basket Room was strictly an after-hours establishment which always had great jam sessions. The Elks Hall had all kinds of concerts and dances. Both the San Pedro Club and the Hole in the Wall had policies of dancing and partying. Unless we were working at a club that paid a guarantee to our band, most of these dates were played for the money at the door.

I'll never forget one incident at the Hole in the Wall. It was just a small beer joint with sawdust on the floor and no bandstand, down from the Lincoln Theater on Central Avenue. The piano and the whole band were on the floor right there with the people. There were no mikes or anything, but one night Sweetpea Robinson and Eric Dolphy got to blowing and battling for chorus after chorus on *Sippin' with Cisco*, which was written for our valet Cisco, since he drank wine like water. This battle of the alto saxes must have lasted damn near an hour. Then after Eric and Sweetpea finished Joe Howard and Hadley Caliman did the same thing. The Hole in the Wall was on fire that night! Those kind of things made it all worth while even when the money wasn't happening.

At the Elks Auditorium on another night during that period, after we finished playing our hearts out, the promoter ran off with the cash box. Consequently I couldn't pay any of the cats in the band. Art Farmer was so mad he wanted to fight me. He told me never to call him again for gigs, rehearsals or anything. He was really angry, but it wasn't my fault. Anyway, I called him two days later about a rehearsal for a gig that weekend. When he came to the telephone his first words were "What do you want mother . . .?" And he was using that big, heavy, gruff, angry voice. I told him about the gig and he said, "Fuck you, Roy." I didn't even call anyone else to take his place because I knew he would be there. Sure enough, come gig time, there he was. Just pure love, my main man. I love him.

I loved every person that had anything to do with that band. When Damita Jo joined the band she was still in high school and was so young and foxy fine that I had to get written permission from her parents for her to appear with the big band. She could really sing too. She didn't stay that long because Joe Adams the disc jockey had eyes for her and she figured he could do more for her than I could. So Joe cornered her. Eventually Damita Jo went off with Steve Gibson's Red Caps, a pleasant lounge group.

The nucleus of the big band was set by this time. Replacements were constantly being made, but not in most key positions. It was no sweat to call for a second trumpet, third alto, or trombone player for any given gig. The mainstays were always there. The band that recorded for Savoy Records consisted of Joe Howard, Clifford Solomon, Eric Dolphy, Leroy "Sweetpea" Robinson and Clyde Dunn on saxophones; Art Farmer, Eddie Preston, Robert Ross and Kenneth Metlock on trumpets; William "Wiggie" Wiginton, Jimmy Knepper and Danny Horton on trombones; Joe Harrison on piano; Addison Farmer and Roger Alderson on bass; Benny White on guitar; Alvy Kidd on congas; Roy Porter on drums; and Paul Sparks on vocals.

We were now playing weekends and rehearsing at the San Pedro Club on San Pedro and Jefferson Boulevard. Jerry Sparks, Paul's older brother, started to manage the band and set up a tour that would take us into Chicago via some of the southern states. Jerry had booked dates in Arizona, Texas and Oklahoma already. I wasn't fortunate enough to have a bus so we were traveling in three automobiles and we had a panel truck for the instruments.

We left on a Friday night from the San Pedro Club to play a one-nighter in Phoenix, Arizona, the next night. We played the Phoenix Auditorium Saturday night and it went very well: a nice crowd and the music was sounding strong. I had to hire another trombone player named Herman Relf in Phoenix because we were one horn short. That next Monday we left for El Paso, Texas. When we got near Deming, New Mexico, the highway had some "soft shoulders" and the car had a blowout doing 80 miles an hour. Art Farmer, Clyde Dunn and I were taken to hospital in Deming but at the time, since we were in shock, we didn't realize that the car had turned over three times. Cisco and the driver didn't get a scratch. Art and Clyde both had concussion and I had four ribs broken. We were in the hospital in Deming about one week.

The band went on trying to get replacements along the route but to no avail. They played El Paso, Texas, and Lawton, Oklahoma, but had to cancel dates farther on. They did get to play a dance in Hobbs, New Mexico, on the way back. Art, Clyde and I were released from the hospital and met the band in Hobbs. I must say this, within a half hour after the accident Hunter Hancock was broadcasting about the occurrence on the radio station where he was working.

We all returned to Los Angeles together. We were disappointed, naturally, but very lucky. I was able to recuperate at the Wadsworth VA Hospital in Westwood because I am a veteran of World War II. I didn't really realize how popular the band was until I started receiving all kinds of get-well and good wishes cards while there – all due to Hunter Hancock, Bill Sampson and Charles Trammell's radio shows. It was a very good feeling. I was astounded so many people liked the band and that it had so many fans, mostly because of Hunter Hancock, because more people listened to him than to the others. When I got out of the hospital, Hunter came to my home for a special interview on his "Harlem Matinee" radio show. I never forgot that.

I was able to get the band back together but it was never the same. I guess the accident had taken its toll. We were rehearsing one day at the Club Alabam and a gentleman by the name of Mr Henry Smith walked in and listened for a while. He gave me his card and said he was an A & R man for Knockout Records. I hadn't heard of Knockout, but he asked me very sincerely if I would like to record four sides for him. At the time I didn't know he actually owned the company, but it made me feel good. Here was a black record company wanting to record a big band. We recorded one afternoon in a studio out in Glendale, but I can't remember the exact date or the name of the studio. We recorded *Hunter's Hunters*, written by Joe Howard and dedicated to Hunter Hancock; *Sampson's Creep*, by Robert Ross, for Bill Sampson who broadcast from Jack's Basket Room and used *Creep* as a theme for his radio show; *Blues à la Carte*, by Robert Ross, a vocal by Harold Grant; and *Moods at Dusk*, featuring Eric Dolphy as main soloist, but Jimmy Knepper also.

The Knockout session personnel was not the same as at the Savoy sessions, but it was a very good session: Eric Dolphy, Joe Maini, Joe Howard, Hadley Caliman and Anthony Ortega, saxes; Art Farmer, Robert Ross, Kenny Bright and Reuben McFall, trumpets; Jimmy Knepper, William Wiginton and Danny Horton, trombones; Russ Freeman, piano; Addison Farmer, bass; Harold Grant, vocal and guitar; Mike Pacheco, congas; and myself, drums. The sides were released, but due to lack of distribution were unheard of. Ironically all masters of Knockout Records were destroyed by fire at a storage plant.

As far as my relationship with Eric Dolphy is concerned, the first day that Eric walked into rehearsals I felt that he was a different breed of individual. But what I didn't know at that particular time was that he was a practiceaholic and studied *all the time*. All I knew was that he was attending LA City College. So what? A little later I found out that at his home with his parents he had a small practice studio where he could and did literally practice around the clock. Eric came from a more affluent family than most of the rest of the guys in the band. Private teachers, and any instruments which he chose, were provided by Mr and Mrs Dolphy. They were behind his musical career all the way. During those early years Eric studied with Buddy Collette, Lloyd Reese, and Mrs Hightower.

Eric Dolphy was dead serious about his future as a musician even at that point. All bands have groupies and ours was no exception. At all gigs and rehearsals, especially the Chicken Shack ones, loads of fine young broads would be hanging around hitting on the cats. But not Eric. When rehearsal was over he would pack up his horns and go home and practice some more. The rest of the cats were saying, "This shit is cool." But Eric didn't have time for no dilly-dallying around. The other musicians would ask, "What's wrong with this sucker, is he crazy?" Yet Eric was right, the chicks and the hangers-on did become distractions at the rehearsals. So we started having closed rehearsals. Finally Eric saw that I was serious about trying to keep the band together and he started to open up to me. When he told me that one of his ambitions was to be among the first black musicians to play in the LA Philharmonic Orchestra, I had to respect him because I did not read music very well then, though I had a hell of an ear. I asked Eric to take over the saxophone section and mold it, which he did in short order. Art Farmer had the brass section under control and I had the rhythm section moving. It all worked out beautifully. We started rehearsing in sections: Mondays – the saxes; Wednesdays – brass section; and on Thursday and Friday we'd put the whole band together. That's one of the reasons the band was so tight.

I'll admit there were a few pill heads, heavy wine drinkers and those who were chippying with heroin, but it didn't impede the progress of the band. It was not riddled with junkies. There were two or three guys that were using, but no one in the band at that time was strung out. I was dropping pills and drinking wine myself.

The band was fairly well disciplined under these circumstances. We had no financial backers or people like Billy Shaw or William Morris booking us, so we did the best we could. I had Wiggie Wiginton handling the band's business and all I really had to do was lead the band and play drums.

By and by I noticed Eric bringing clarinets and flutes to rehearsals and experimenting. He was a special young man. But Sweetpea Robinson was the star on alto saxophone and took most of the solos. Eric later went on, of course, to make a name for himself in New York playing all the reed instruments. I think that became more important to him than being in the LA Philharmonic Orchestra, and indeed he did become one of the legends of the saxophone and made people aware of the possibilities of the bass clarinet and flute in jazz. For the record, Eric Dolphy is featured on both *Gassin' the Wig* and *Little Wig*.

The big band certainly had its share of tough times in its short life, but I am sure that I am not alone in remembering the joys and happiness that all connected with this venture experienced. It was purely a labor of love on everyone's part. The band was an institution of learning for me and all concerned. It launched the careers of quite a few musicians. My regret is that the public never really became aware of that particular big band, although I am pleased that it is partially preserved on vinyl. Most of all I am proud to have been a part of it.

After the Knockout recording session in early 1950, the decline of my big band was inevitable. I decided to take a hiatus from Los Angeles, so off to Oakland I went with Sonny Criss to work the Wolf Club. My intentions were to return to Los Angeles at the end of that engagement and re-form the big band. But things didn't work out that way.

6

Lonesome Mood

After I got busted in March of 1953 in San Francisco, I did almost three months' dead time in County Jail before I was sent to the San Quentin Guidance Center in June. Me and Mary broke up when I got popped, but she told me that she would look out for my drums, clothing and other belongings. Some time later when she came to see me in Chino she told me that all of my things were in storage.

In the meantime she married some dude who was a captain in the army. I didn't blame her for getting married since the changes that I had taken her through as a junkie were horrendous. But for a woman who was supposed to be my lady, to make a trip to prison with the sole purpose of showing me her wedding pictures just seemed a little too cold. I guess she called that hurting me, though I didn't really give a damn because I sure didn't have marrying eyes.

After that I didn't see Mary again for many years until the late 1960s. She came into the Club Oasis then, when I was working that room for a couple of weeks with Johnny Otis. Unfortunately, she seemed quite disturbed mentally and told me that she had caught her husband in bed with another man. I don't know whether Mary is dead or alive today. I often wonder just whatever happened to her.

After spending three months in San Quentin, I was sent to Chino. There I got a chance to study chord structure, harmony, instrumentation, voicing and arranging. At school they had all kinds of classes: welding, plumbing, carpentry, plastering, etc. They were mostly designed to develop skills that would enhance a person's chances to get and hold a job after they were released. You could also earn a high-school diploma there.

But what was of most interest to me was that they had a hell of a band down there. For a conductor they had a man on staff who was originally from Boston named Daniel Heistand. He was a hell of a musician and also played flute. He was the musical instructor and led the concert band. We played a good deal of Aaron Copland, Stravinsky, Ravel and Tchaikovsky, who became one of my favorite classical composers. I enjoyed Tchaikovsky's music because he had so much soul and because he used minor keys quite frequently in his compositions.

At Chino I learned how to read a bit of music and score music. This educational experience was quite positive because I also had a chance to learn and explore the greats of European classical music. This has stuck with me to this day.

When I arrived at Chino a lot of my friends were already there: Dexter Gordon; Little Ricky White, a baritone sax player; Hadley Caliman, the strong tenor man who'd been in my big band; Paul Sparks, my vocalist from the big band; a white boy by the name of Chris who was an arranger, pianist and trumpet player; and another white boy who was a strong alto saxophonist, Fred Waters. Dexter organized a jazz band, more precisely a bebop band, which was bad, and we put on quite a few concerts there at the mess hall. There'd be Hadley Caliman and later Prince Harrison on tenor sax, Ricky White on baritone, Dex, and myself, and some cats in the rhythm section. It was a swinging outfit. When friends and family would come by on Sundays to visit we'd play out on the recreation yard. We'd generally get to play during the entire visiting period so we'd get in a good couple of solid hours, which was a gas.

In early 1955 they made a movie in Chino. They called it *Unchained*. It was a Hal Bartlett production with a music score by Alex North. The movie featured Elroy "Crazy Legs" Hirsch, the Rams football star, Todd Duncan, a black concert singer, Chester Morris, Barbara Hale and others. Basically it was the story of the Chino Institute for Men, and why one man escaped. Our band appeared without pay in a few scenes as prisoners in the prison band. It wasn't much of a part because the music we played was never used, so it was never heard on the screen. The producers in their infinite wisdom chose to use a dixieland soundtrack instead.

I did two years there at Chino. They weren't really bad years, just long ones. I did, as mentioned, learn to write music, and I developed a more sophisticated attitude towards all music. In addition, the exposure to European classical music was positive. So they were productive years.

The mandatory provisions for parole are that you have a steady job upon release and that you do not associate with your old "friends," or that environment, which got you into the joint in the first place. I'd worked with Benny Carter before so I wrote him a letter asking if he would verify some type of employment for me so I could get out and hit the bricks. Shit, he didn't even bother to reply. Finally, Don Johnson, a bandleader and former trumpet player with Johnny Otis, answered my letter. He said, "Roy, I'll send a letter of employment for you but I have a regular drummer. Still, at least you'll get out on the streets this way." Don did just that and I have never forgotten that kindness. I guess I can understand the reluctance of people to get involved with me because very few addicts kick for good. The saying "Once a hype – always a hype" is damn near true. The trouble was that I *knew* I was through with heroin forever, even if the other people did not.

When I was released from Chino I made a special trip up to San Francisco during the Christmas season of 1955 to get my drums, my clothes and the rest of my belongings. My landlady in LA, Molly Singleton, was driving to San Francisco to visit and offered me the ride. Molly was like a mother to me, since I'd lived there at her apartment building at Vernon and Crocker before I moved to San Francisco in 1950. She was always so good to me. When I was leading the big band, money was often a problem. If I had the rent that was fine, and if I didn't that was fine too. Molly knew that I'd always make it up to her. She was also helpful when I first got out of the joint, since that 40 dollars that they give doesn't go far. But when I got to the storage place in Frisco, the people there told me that all my possessions had been sold to pay for the storage bill. I didn't have a set of drums even if I got a gig!

I was really discouraged then until Johnny Kirkwood laid some old drums on me. Right after that, from totally out of the blue, Joe Liggins called me and offered me a job playing with him at a club in the Inglewood section of Los Angeles called The Tailspin. I worked there with Joe and the Honeydrippers for about four weeks. Thanks to Joe I started to get back on my feet.

I was pretty shocked when Joe called me to make this gig. I was known as a bebop drummer and Joe was one of the kings of rhythm and blues, so it seemed like an unlikely pairing. The job worked out fine, though, and I am glad I did take the work because it opened my eyes to that style of music.

After we closed at The Tailspin I moved from Molly's apartments to another place on 35th Street, near Maple Avenue. This was in early 1956. Then Jack McVea hired me for a job with his band at the Club Royal in San Diego. Jack McVea is a tenor saxophonist who had a big hit record with *Open the Door Richard*, a tune made famous by the great comedian Dusty Fletcher. We were in San Diego between six and eight weeks. While with McVea there I first heard Harold Land, the great tenor man, and the drummer Leon Petties. They were both working in a band in another club not too far from the Club Royal. From San Diego we went on to Tucson, Arizona. There we played another club for about six weeks and then came back to Los Angeles.

All the band members with McVea drank wine like water and so I started drinking wine also. Maybe my bad nerves had something to do with it. Actually, this was just one more thing, since I had started drinking and popping pills almost as soon as I got out of Chino in December 1955.

Later in 1956, after the work with McVea, I went into the Club Sirocco, which later became Donte's, on Lankershim Boulevard. I was playing drums again for Joe Liggins, and we packed people in night after night there at the Sirocco for three months. This was a great gig as far as the music was concerned but the owner of the club was something else.

Chuck Boyd was such a racist that he had the audacity to tell Joe that the band had to come in through the kitchen in the back. Joe told him to kiss his ass. Well, the club stayed packed with fans so Boyd retracted this order and promptly renewed our contract. Truth was that Boyd was making a grand theft of dough off us.

These opportunities to work with Joe Liggins caused me to have nothing but the utmost admiration and respect for him. To this day I don't think most people have any idea what a great musician he is. There aren't many others who have composed more hit songs than Joe.

Rene Bloch, who'd been in my big band, was playing lead alto and was straw boss with Perez Prado's mambo band. He called and asked me to join their band. Perez was a big name in early 1957 with hit records like *Cherry Pink and Apple Blossom White* for RCA. I really only had a short stay with Perez, but it was quite enjoyable. We played a few one-nighters, and ended up down at the Orpheum Theater at 9th and Broadway in downtown Los Angeles. (Other theaters that booked big bands with stage shows included the Paramount, between Broadway and Hill; Loew's State on 8th and Hill; the Million Dollar on 3rd and Broadway; and the Lincoln Theater at 22nd and Central Avenue.)

This period in my musical education was quite exciting, and playing with Perez opened my eyes to the great sounds of authentic Latin rhythms. During this time I had the good fortune to play with one of the greatest conga players in the world, Armando Peraza. He was a real inspiration and I had a ball working with this master in that big band. I really enjoyed the sounds the band made with the repetitions of the rhythms and the shrieking of those four saxes, three trumpets and one trombone. That type of stuff got to me. I even had an opportunity to travel with Prado abroad to Europe, but I regret to say that I didn't go.

During the engagement at the Orpheum Theater with Prado I met a man who was to play an important role in my life. By this point my drinking and dropping pills had thoroughly screwed up my nerves. Dr Kim was a physician of Korean descent with offices located on Jefferson Boulevard, just around the corner from where I lived. He was always pleasant and didn't make a lot of moral judgements about my life. In addition, it was convenient to see him. Dr Kim told me that because of my addiction to heroin that my body needed building back up. So he started giving me intravenous injections of vitamins. That worked out quite well. In fact, when I was appearing in Los Angeles at shows such as Prado's at the Orpheum, I'd hop in my car between sets and go to his office for these vitamin injections. The most important thing Kim told me was not to drink alcohol because I would definitely become an alcoholic. I did not heed his advice. Fool that I was, I did not stop my drinking.

Eventually, Dr Kim put me on Miltown, the first amphetamine drug that I had heard about. It is a tranquilizer and an anti-depressant. Since then I've had just about any kind of nerve or upper and downer pill you can name. Previously I'd snorted coke, shot morphine, shot heroin, shot speedballs of coke and heroin. And, despite Dr Kim's admonitions, I ended up an alcoholic just as he predicted.

As I've been suffering from tremendous migraine headaches since the early 1950s, a variety of doctors have had me on some form of medication for years. But I could get no relief from these headaches even with all of the medications, so I would drink for relief right along with the pills. This was strictly taboo and soon that shit was to take its toll.

In the late 1950s I began another association with a man who ended up teaching me a great deal. One day I received a call from the producer Robert "Bumps" Blackwell. He wanted me to do a demo record with a singing piano player whom he had brought to Los Angeles from Macon, Georgia. The pianist's name was Richard Penniman. We went into a recording studio in a garage owned by a bass player named Ted Brinson. There, at 28th Street near Cimarron Avenue, we recorded some songs which Mr Penniman had written.

Penniman, of course, became famous as Little Richard. His stardom was due in no small part to the promotional genius of Bumps Blackwell.

Bumps liked my drumming and so he called me a bit later to do another session with the Soul Stirrers, a gospel group. At the time Sam Cooke was a member of the Soul Stirrers and he was sounding very strong in that context too. I remember this session well because it was the first time I had been told to bring only one stick, snare drum and bass drum to a recording session. All Bumps wanted was a two and four back-beat with the stick on the snare, rim-shot style. Eventually, just as he did with Little Richard, Bumps made Sam Cooke into a star. Bumps was a strong influence on my life and career. I didn't know then just how big of an influence he was to have on me as a man, producer and musician, but I was soon to find that out and I went on to work with him a bit later.

I continued to keep up on my writing and found myself going back to some things I had composed while I was away at Chino. Among these pieces was a drum piece called *On the Street of Drums*, which Chico Hamilton used as a title for something he did. A friend of mine who was a hell of a singer kept after me about some of my songs. His name was Jesse Belvin and he was quite interested for a time in some instrumentals called *Wow, Love You, Got a Funny Feelin'* and *Minor Mood*, which was to become famous later as *Lonesome Mood*. Soon, however, Jesse's record company was to take him in another direction. And while he never did do anything with these songs of mine which he liked, he did go on to become one of the best vocalists of that era.

Henry Smith was the next man on the scene who wanted to record me. Henry had recorded my big band in 1950 for Knockout Records. After hearing these new tunes he promptly decided to record me for his new label, Debonair Records, which he'd formed in 1956 with Carl Leftwich. Henry set up a session where I played piano and organ along with Sonny Criss on alto, Buddy Woodson on bass and Al Bartee on drums. We did *Minor Mood* with piano, *Wow* on organ, while *Love You* and *Got a Funny Feelin'* were done with vocals and organ. These were pressed and released as 78s but never received the right kind of airplay or distribution, and so nothing much happened.

In the meantime I was playing at the Rag Doll nightclub on Victory and Lankershim in North Hollywood. The group was led by Sigmund Galloway on tenor sax, with Henry McDade on piano and Clora Bryant on trumpet and vocals. This was my first experience working with Clora, but I could tell that she would someday leave her mark on the music scene. She could play fine trumpet and was a talented singer and was very foxy.

During the course of the night on the stand at the Rag Doll Louis Jordan came by to listen to my drumming. This came about through a friend of mine, Devonia "Lady Dee" Williams. Devonia, a pianist, was back in New York City with Johnny Otis and had run into Louis Jordan. They got to talking and he mentioned that he was looking for a good drummer when he came out to the West Coast for a tour. Devonia mentioned my name, but Louis wasn't sure that I would work out because of my using past and since I was known as a bebop drummer. Devonia said that I wasn't a junkie any longer and that I was playing all kinds of music. Finally, after she assured him that I was clean, he agreed to come by and listen to my playing when he hit Los Angeles.

So when Louis Jordan walked through the door I had it worked out with Sig that we would play something with a shuffle and back-beat similar to the style of music which Louis played. The evening went well and Sig was such a help that Louis told me he liked my playing and asked me if I'd like to go out on the road with him. He explained that he was moving out to Phoenix, Arizona, for his health and would be doing quite a bit of work out in the west. I said great, and then all I had to do was clear it with my parole officer.

Since I was on parole I had to have written permission to travel outside of Los Angeles. Luckily, my parole officer was a real swinging dude, originally from Canada. I've forgotten his name but he was very easy-going about my traveling with Louis. The parole officer even invited me to his home on holidays, but I never did make that. He was a character, and when he'd come by the house to check in on me, we'd listen to music and he'd fire up a joint and shoot the breeze. He was real supportive of my music and me getting back on the track, and every gig I had he'd always show up with his wife and stay for most all of the show. It was a beautiful relationship for a parolee and a parole officer.

Up to this point Louis Jordan had always been billed as Louis Jordan and his Tympany Five, but when I was hired he'd changed the personnel completely. Now he had a lounge act and he featured Jackie Davis on organ, Austin Powell on guitar, who'd made a name for himself in the Cats and a Fiddle group, and a female vocalist named Marjorie, who also played congas, which bugged the hell out of me because she just wasn't that good a player.

My work with Louis Jordan worked out well enough. He told me not to play bebop and to just shuffle along and stay clean. I did just that. In fact, I became an expert at it. We rehearsed for about two weeks in Phoenix.

Jordan paid me more money than anybody in jazz ever had. He started me out at 250 dollars a week and then raised it to 300 before I left. He was without doubt one of the greatest showmen I've ever had the pleasure of working with. When we worked Las Vegas in 1957 he didn't play just the lounges, he played the main showroom. We were at the Copa Room in the Sands Hotel with Antonio Morelli's 30-piece pit band behind us. Howard Keel was the star of the show and a young comedian named Joey Bishop was the opening act. It was a gas. Work there at the Sands Hotel was great because we went on stage at the Copa Room at 8.30 p.m. The first show lasted until 9 p.m., then we were off until 12.30 a.m., and the evening was over by 1 a.m. That was it. In between shows and after work I went to the black neighborhood and played keno in the casinos there on the strip. Black musicians couldn't even stay at the hotels they were working in the 1950s.

In addition to the Sands date we played a string of

one-nighters on a double bill with B. B. King. On the night that we played the Oakland Auditorium, there were so many people packed in there it looked like sardines in a can. I had never seen that many people together in one place in my life. But I got tired of always having to play *Caldonia, Let the Good Times Roll* and *One-eyed Fish, Peepin' Through a Sea-food Store,* and so I just split. It was a great experience, though, because it did open other doors, but I really wanted to write.

While I was in Las Vegas with Louis Jordan, I met and married Tina Cecelia Collins. Ms Collins was writing keno tickets at the Cotton Club there and I was quite impressed by her beauty and poise. After I got around to introducing myself she informed me that she knew who I was, since she had met me earlier at Jack's Basket Room on Central Avenue in Los Angeles at a jam session. After a bit of small talk, she showed me how to play keno tickets in such a way that if I did hit I would have a nice taste. We started playing together as partners and my luck changed. I asked her, "Will you marry me with your delicious candy self?" She smiled and said, "Hell, no."

Then I asked her to come see the show at the Sands. She promised that she would but she never came by. I thought, "Damn, I must be losing my touch." When I finally caught up with her again, I asked her to come to see me at the motel, which she did. I asked her to marry me and she said yes. We were married the next day, on 27 January 1957, at a Justice of the Peace office in Vegas. I left town the next day and she came on to Los Angeles. From this union we have a son, Daryl Roy Porter, who was born on 4 June 1959.

One of the things I always admired in Tina was her sense of loyalty. When we first got together, all her friends were saying, "Once a junkie, always a junkie." But she just told them to mind their own business, she had so much faith in me. Although we were divorced in 1968, she has written lyrics to many of my songs. In fact, we recently completed a beautiful ballad called *Time for Dreams.* Together we own Rotine Music Company, which is an ASCAP publishing business, and to this day we remain the best of friends.

In 1958, after forming Rotine Music, I changed my song

Minor Mood to *Lonesome Mood* when I added lyrics to the music. I didn't do much with that song then because the climate didn't seem right. The Central Avenue scene had long since moved on. The new hot spots were on the west side in Hollywood, Santa Monica and Hermosa Beach, or in the valley near the movie studios. There weren't too many record dates for black jazz musicians because the "West Coast" or "cool" jazz sound was coming in. White musicians had a field day through the 1960s because this was their sound. Black jazz artists were left out in the cold because this so-called cool school of playing was too narrow a category for us to fit into.

Earl Bostic got in touch with me during this time, wanting me to play in his band. I took the job, which was a real eye-opener. Bostic was a great musician and a total monster on alto sax. I knew he was bad, but I didn't know he was as great as he was. Earl also learned to play guitar very well and doubled on that instrument. But for drummers, Earl always had to have a back-beat going at all times on all tunes. This is what sold his records, along with his sound on alto. One night in Portland, Oregon, he showed me how to play a double shuffle with a back-beat. I'd been doing a single shuffle with the right hand on the cymbal, while the left hand was doing a back-beat on two and four. The double is with both hands shuffling, keeping the back-beat going too. No easy task at some tempos, but it makes for a heavier beat. He was an amazing musician.

His band included John Anderson, trumpet; Jewel Grant, baritone saxophone; Teddy Edwards, tenor saxophone; Adolphus Alsbrook, bass; Charles Martin, piano; Irving Ashby, guitar; Bill Jones, vocals; and myself on drums. It was a very dynamic band which produced some very enjoyable music. I recorded an album with Bostic for King records entitled *Earl Bostic's Greatest Hits*, which came out fairly well.

After this venture I got into my writing again and that was when I added words to *Minor Mood*. In 1959 I took the vocal group The Chromatics, led by Chuck and Helen Level, into the studio and recorded a demo record of *Lonesome Mood*. It came out so well and sounded quite fine, and when Larry Green and The Titans heard it they promptly recorded it for Richard Bock's World Pacific Jazz label. The song was released but it wasn't pushed.

I then recorded four sides for Rudy Harvey's Amazon Records label – *Good Cookin'*, *Summer Night*, *You Do this to Me* and *Juicy*. Harvey was also a DJ over at KGFJ radio, which at that time was located over on Sunset and Vine. They were playing *Good Cookin'* pretty regularly, but one night Harvey turned the record over and played the flip side. All of a sudden *Juicy* became a hit and people started calling in requesting it. The song did so well that I was able to make the down payment on my house thanks to it. Ironically, I happened to be playing piano on the song.

Claude McLin, the great saxophonist who plays somewhat in that hard-hitting Gene Ammons style, and who's also a talented vocalist, called me about this time. So I started working with McLin at the Trocadero Supper Club at Florence and Figueroa. McLin was out of Chicago and had assembled a first-rate band, including Paul Bryant on organ, Sonny Kenner on guitar and myself on drums. After closing at the Trocadero we went on to the Club Intimé, which had been the old Hi-De-Ho Club. We played there at 50th and Western for about four weeks and everyone that heard us got their ears full of good music.

John McClain hired us after that to play his It Club on Washington, near La Brea. McLin knocked 'em out there too, with his Jug style and his singing too. The last time I saw Claude McLin was in 1969 or 1970. He had given up music completely, which was a crying shame since he was really a damn good musician.

A nice thing came out of all this work for McLin when one night at the It Club, around 1963, Rex Middleton stopped by. I knew Rex as a singer and pianist, but that was about it. He said that he had heard The Titan's version of *Lonesome Mood* and wanted to record it with his vocal group. I didn't believe him. Most of the people that I had submitted the song to had rejected it, saying that it was too modern for the day or wasn't for them. They gave me all kinds of excuses, which by the time Middleton came along I had gotten used to hearing.

For example, my wife Tina had sent a lead sheet and tape along to both the Four Freshmen and The Hi-Lo's, thinking that it would be perfect for either one of them because it had their type of harmonic structure. Sure enough, both groups liked it. In about a week or two The Hi-Lo's manager told me over the phone to come by his office and we'd sign a contract because they definitely wanted to record it. When I walked through the door of their office on Vine Street, racism reared its ugly head. They reneged and told me that they would get back in touch with me. They never did. I suppose that, because they hadn't seen me before and didn't realize that I was black, they didn't realize who they were dealing with. I know that that song was not a typical black sound, so maybe this threw them.

Anyway, so when Rex Middleton came along expressing interest in the song, I was sceptical, even though he was black. But Middleton was true to his word and a little later he recorded it for Ray Charles's Tangerine Records. It received some national exposure at that point. In fact, I have to give Red Middleton credit for the song ever becoming a hit. This was in 1964 and after that it lay dormant for a number of years.

Later in 1964 Joe Liggins opened at the Harrah's Club in Lake Tahoe. Joe was on organ, I was on drums, and the other member of the trio was a guitar player from back east whose name eludes me. We opened the night Cassius Clay beat Sonny Liston for the heavyweight boxing championship of the world.

Our trio was backing a folk-gospel group called the Jubilee Four. We played the lounge at Harrah's for 45-minute sets along with Louis Prima, George Rock and other lounge acts that were at the top of that circuit. Sammy Davis was featured in the main room and when he'd finish his set he'd come over and sit in with us and play drums. One night he hit a 25,000 dollar jackpot ticket on keno, which was the limit, but he'd probably played that much up anyway.

Across the street from Harrah's is Harvey's Hotel, where Stanley Morgan and his Inkspots group were appearing. They were over there with Esquivel and his big band. Esquivel was bad. I think this was the first time I had heard electronics used in a big band.

Joe Liggins's trio was at Harrah's for four weeks and when we left I was totally broke. I had been playing keno and eventually had to hock my camera to Joe to pay my rent. Although I enjoyed playing with that trio, the gig did me no good financially. The night we closed Billy Eckstine opened along with Edie Adams, who was married at that time to Ernie Kovacs, in the main show room at Harrah's.

Charles Gray, a cocktail drummer, was also leading an Inkspots group, of which there are many, and he gave me a call to do a month's worth of work in Northern California in Vallejo. Teddy Bunn, my former boss and one of the all time greats on guitar, was in that band. Teddy was beginning to lose his sight at that point and shortly thereafter he went completely blind.

On one of our off nights, I decided to call Rose Brame, an old girlfriend of mine in San Francisco whom I used to live with during the Bop City days. She told me to come on over and see all the changes that had hit San Francisco. I couldn't believe my eyes when I got there. All of the great jazz clubs that were there in 1957 when I'd last been up there were torn down for either parking lots or freeways. Even Bop City was no more. Progress.

When we came back home to Los Angeles at the end of 1964, Clifton White gave me a call. White, who was a guitarist and who'd been Sam Cooke's musical director, wanted me to join a trio at the Hacienda Hotel in El Segundo. I took the job and it turned out to be quite an educational experience. White was leading a guitar trio with Jerry Harmon on piano, who was later replaced by John Rodby, and myself on drums.

At the Hacienda this was a strictly show type of gig. I'd played shows before on the Apollo Theatre circuit and elsewhere, but this was much different, almost like the shows that are in Las Vegas. An evening's entertainment featured flamenco acts, can-can dancers, Russian Volga dancers, Tahitian dancers and other shows. These were all major productions. One I remember particularly well was a very professional rendition of Kurt Weill's *Lost in the Stars*. Our trio played for three of these shows during the course of the evening. Another group played for dancing. Quite an experience. These shows were produced by Bumps Blackwell and they were truly incredible. It was a completely new education for me because each act had its own authentic music written down in arrangement form. The shows changed every six weeks and it was a constant challenge for three musicians to keep such shows moving like clockwork. The money was far and away the best I've ever made on any job in Los Angeles. We stayed there for three years.

During those three years at the Hacienda I really got exposed to a cross-section of entertainers. During those productions you knew that some of those people were going to go on to bigger things. One of them was Poupee, a beautiful foxy flamenco dancer that ended up doing movies and appearing in television commercials. A singing duo, Kevin and Gregg, reminded me of the Righteous Brothers, and were just as talented, but they broke up before they hit pay dirt. I'm not certain what happened to a dancer named Jamaica Joe, but when he did his limbo act he'd break up the house night after night. Marilyn McCoo worked in that show for quite a while. Beverly Sanders, who later did television shows and commercials, worked the Hacienda as a singer and dancer. There I heard one of the greatest jazz singers, a woman named Sallie Blair. She was beautiful and when she walked on stage you could hear a pin drop. She had more stage presence than many big-name singers. The only thing that kept Sallie Blair from making it to the top was an alcohol problem.

The Watts riots broke out during the summer of 1965 and it was pretty hot throughout the south-eastern section of Los Angeles. It was "Burn Baby Burn" time. This affected many people that had jobs where they had to go into or through the area to get to work. People that lived west of Crenshaw

Boulevard could not easily get to the east side of Los Angeles. I was living four blocks west of Crenshaw on Virginia Road and worked in El Segundo at the Hacienda, which was near the LA International Airport. So for me this didn't present a problem. But the LA police had a field day during those stormy times, beating, killing and taking just about anyone they wanted into jail. I had my own little run-in with the police then, too.

It was a Monday night and we were off from the Hacienda. I got into my car and drove to a bar on Exposition Boulevard near Arlington Avenue. When I sat down at the bar and ordered a Budweiser, I noticed a man watching me from the other end of the bar. Now, I'm messed up on pills and juice anyway, so I get paranoid after a few more drinks because the dude looks like a white boy. I'm sitting there getting madder and madder thinking about the riot situation. I'm really starting to flip about why this cat is in a black bar anyway, while his white police brothers are killing my people. So I started to see red. I asked him why he was staring at me. He said that he was not staring at me and sure enough one word led to another. The barmaid called the police and I got arrested for disturbing the peace. When they took me outside they found a ten-inch switchblade knife on me and took my ass down to Lincoln Heights jail.

Lincoln Heights had been condemned and closed, but during the Watts riots period it was opened back up to put all of the black people in there who were arrested. The police had people packed in there like sardines. There were people in there crowding the cells, the tanks and even the walkways. The plumbing hadn't worked for years and just getting drinking water was a major problem. I saw people drink water out of toilet bowls.

After a couple of days I went up before a woman judge and explained that I used the knife to clean fish with when I went fishing. She didn't really buy that, but she let me off with paying a fine for disturbing the peace. The cops had taken my knife and broken the blade anyway.

I'd never seen so many people herded like cattle into the

jails and then into the courtroom. This particular judge probably let me go because she was tired of looking at so many black people at one time. But the final irony to this little sordid incident was that, since my thinking was so impaired from alcohol and pills, the man at the bar that looked Caucasian was not. He was a light-skinned black man.

One of the biggest screw-ups I ever made was on the Hacienda Hotel gig. It too was due to alcohol and pills. Bumps Blackwell had been contacted by Bill Dana, the producer for the "Milton Berle Show," to present our show on Berle's television program. This meant that the hotel would not have one show, because we would all have to be over in Hollywood for the dress rehearsal for Berle. Normally at the Hacienda we did three shows a night, and on Saturdays we did six because of the one o'clock matinee.

A few days before the show aired we went up to the theater, which is now the Palace on Vine Street, for the first rehearsal. I always kept an extra set of drums in the trunk of my car for just such occasions, so this was no problem. I even took my five-year-old son Daryl along to the rehearsal. This was a gas because Milton Berle and all the cast members were making over him, taking pictures, etc. This was nice, but it didn't affect Daryl too much one way or the other because he's always been quite level-headed about celebrities.

This rehearsal was in the day on Monday. Our dress rehearsal was for Thursday night and the show was set for Friday evening. We all made the dress rehearsal and everything went fine. I even got the chance to meet the great Bette Davis, who happened to be a guest on the show.

After the rehearsal I stopped off at a bar on the way back home and had a couple of drinks and that was it. When it was all over people told me that I was in and out of a beer joint on 54th Street for three days. I'd missed the "Milton Berle Show" on national TV and hadn't called anyone to let them know where I was or what was going on. I had blacked out. Talk about feeling bad, embarrassed and ashamed. That was me.

I called Cliff White to see if I still had the gig at the Hacienda and he said yes. He understood what I was going through with the headaches and medication. They had replaced me for Berle's show with one of the top studio drummers, Alvin Stoller. I felt terrible because I'd told a lot of friends about our television appearance and I didn't even show.

When I finally got to work a couple of nights later I couldn't even look anyone in the eye, I was so ashamed. That show that Bumps had there at the Hacienda was so professional and so intricate that it wasn't easy to get a drummer to come in and play it like I did it. I was later told that that was the only reason that I wasn't fired. I asked myself, "Damn, Roy, you're 43 years old and still fucking up. When will it end?" But Bumps Blackwell never gave up on me. For that reason and many others I have always loved and admired him a great deal.

Robert "Bumps" Blackwell was a native of Seattle, Washington. He had a brother, Charlie, who is a drummer and singer that is still active in that area. Their mother was a very kind woman whom I knew quite well all the way up until her death when she was over 80 years old. Bumps had a daughter, Sandy, who lives here in Los Angeles, is married and has two children.

Bumps was a master musician who was adept on many instruments, as well as being a first-rate arranger and voice teacher. He was the one who got Quincy Jones started on his musical career. Bumps gave Quincy quite a few pointers about his trumpet playing and his writing. And he was responsible for the successful careers of many other people within the music world. He gave Sam Cooke, Lou Rawls and Little Richard their first breaks. He also looked after the career of the famous gospel singer Bessie Griffin. At one time or other Bumps managed all of these artists.

I worked with Bessie Griffin on a number of occasions, the first time being at a Soul Stirrers gospel recording session at a studio on Fairfax, north of Beverly Boulevard, in the 1950s. Sam Cooke was also in that group.

Unfortunately, over the years most of these people

deserted the man who got them started. Bumps used to tell me how Little Richard would fire him at will until he needed him to straighten out some business deal that his other managers couldn't handle. But at least Little Richard came all the way from London, where he was working, to eulogize Bumps at his funeral.

Bumps was a wonderful person that was taken advantage of by producers – black and white. Art Rupe's Specialty Records would never have become as successful as it did if it had not been for Bumps Blackwell. When Bumps recorded Little Richard and other artists for that label, that was the real beginning of success of Specialty.

Blackwell was one of the pioneering fathers of rock-and-roll producers. He was always equally adept at producing rock, jazz or any kind of music because he knew what he wanted from his musicians, engineers and studio technicians. He was one of the first I knew who used synthesizers to get special sounds such as running water or the sound of a motorcycle. He was way ahead of his time in that department. I learned a great deal about songwriting, producing and recording from Bumps. His life enriched many people and I will never forget all of the things that he passed along to me or what a wonderful and humane person he was.

At this point I was also doing a lot of work with Bobby Day, whom I call Mr Rockin' Robin because of his hit records *Rockin' Robin* and *Little Bitty Pretty One*. His real name is Robert Byrd. Bobby is one of the pioneer singers and showmen of rock-and-roll. For quite a while he had his own revue called the "Bobby Day Show." With this revue I played such spots as the San Diego Civic Auditorium, most of the clubs on the Sunset Strip in Hollywood, and the Five Four Ballroom at 54th and Broadway in LA. Bobby Day was a true entertainer on stage with his choreography and tremendous presence. I remember this period fondly as a beautiful experience, particularly since the style of rock is so much different than jazz.

After my three years at the Hacienda Hotel I began working at a spot on Florence and Van Ness called Mr

Woodley's Nightclub. I was there with a trio which included Tollie Moore Jr on organ and Ray Brooks on guitar. We worked Mr Woodley's matinee show on Sunday, along with shows on Monday and Tuesday nights. Then later in the week, on Friday and Saturday nights, that same trio along with Maurice Simon on tenor saxophone and flute would work the swanky Yamashiro Sky Room in the Hollywood Hills.

I worked these two gigs for quite a while and eventually replaced Brooks on guitar with Chuck Norris, since Ray went on to form his own band. Anyway, as I'd be driving back and forth to work I'd listen to my AM car radio and I kept hearing the Friends of Distinction singing their big hit *Grazin' in the Grass*. Each time I'd hear this group I'd start thinking about how I could get some of my material to them. At that time I didn't have FM radio in my car and I didn't even know that the Friends had recorded *Lonesome Mood* on this same LP, and that my song was being played on the jazz station KBCA FM-105, which became KKGO.

One day I was taking an afternoon snooze and all of a sudden I hear, "Oh yes, you've gone now, what is there for me to do?" I jumped straight up and said, "Damn, that's my tune." I was floored. I called Jai Rich, the DJ that was broadcasting then at KBCA, and asked him who was singing. He told me that it was the Friends of Distinction on RCA records. This was in early 1969. The Friends were half of Rex Middleton's Hi Fi's, while the other part of his group became the Fifth Dimension. At any rate, the Friends of Distinction's first album, *Grazin'*, went gold, selling over a million copies.

Lonesome Mood has a rather strange history since I first thought of the melody while I was incarcerated in San Quentin. Later, while I was doing time at Chino, I put the entire song together with chords and the harmony. Although it gives the impression of being entirely about a woman, it is really about smack and a woman, since at that time I was a junkie and my only true love was heroin. But the Friends of Distinction did my song up grand and it is just a shame that they didn't stay together longer, since they were such a terrific and moving vocal group.

Most people were surprised that I was writing and composing. They were also surprised that this song was written by a drummer, I suppose because of the chord changes and its structural mood. The success of *Lonesome Mood* gave me the incentive to continue with my writing. I said to myself, "Hell, I ain't never made this kind of bread playin' no drums." And while I haven't had a hit like that since, I'm still writing.

I continued my work with the trio at Woodley's for another six months and worked for one year at the Yamashiro Sky Room. I called the group Roy Porter Sounds during that period, and eventually changed it to the Roy Porter Sound Machine when I began to add more horns and other instruments when I recorded the group.

There were a handful of clubs in the late 1960s that were trying to keep the black jazz tradition alive in Los Angeles. You could always hear good sounds at places like the Club La Chris on Avalon Boulevard near 40th, the Town Tavern at 36th Place and Western, the Watkins Hotel (which later became the Rubaiyat Room) at Adams and Western, the Hillcrest Club (which became the Black Orchid) on Washington and Vineyard and John McClain's It Club. Another place where you could see everybody from Dizzy to Brother Jack McDuff was the Parisian Room at Washington and La Brea. In Hollywood there was Shelly's Manne-Hole on Cahuenga Boulevard. And just outside of the city there was The Lighthouse in Hermosa Beach. Another nice little club was called Marty's at 58th Street and Broadway. They had a strong jazz policy and also featured jam sessions. Bert Kendrick's group, featuring William Green – the all around reeds player – was there for quite a while. Marty's later moved to La Brea and Stocker, and became known as Marty's on the Hill. Before folding in the 1970s, it featured quite a few name acts such as Gerald Wilson's big band, Eddie Harris and Gloria Lynne.

A few black musicians were making a good living in the

studios. People like William Green, Buddy Collette, Red Callender and Earl Palmer all did a great deal of work in the recording, motion-picture and television industries. Earl Palmer is from New Orleans and he was one of the few black drummers around doing any kind of studio work. He really had that New Orleans style which I call a "bayou feeling" and could play just about anything you threw at him, from rhythm and blues to rock and jazz. Palmer is quite a talented drummer. Of course, the first black musicians that were hired by the studios were Benny Carter and Lee Young.

In the beginning I had a very emotional feeling that all black musicians that were trying to get into the studio scene were forsaking their musical heritage just to get into an alien environment where they really were not welcome. At that time I called these musicians the intellectual wimps of jazz. It wasn't until somewhat later, after I'd had a chance to really think about it, that I accepted the fact that some of these people were just not innovators and did not have the soul or feeling towards our music. To me this seemed like a sell-out. I finally realized that for these people material things meant more to them than our music. I accept that and am not making a judgement on their actions. All I can say is that for me I couldn't go in that direction because of my own beliefs.

All the while a young man who used to be on the scene listening to the giants of bebop and my big band in the early years was busy honing his skills. At that time I wasn't too aware of him – he was too young to get into the clubs. He left Los Angeles with Ornette Coleman for New York, where he stayed on. When I recall him making a name for himself was on the recording of Lee Morgan's great LP *The Sidewinder* for Blue Note records. In a short time he became practically the house drummer for Blue Note. This was young Billy Higgins, who'd grown up here in LA. "B" had made it, and went on to become the most recorded drummer in jazz, never forgetting or compromising his roots.

7

Sound Machine

The Yamashiro Sky Room is a part of a large Japanese-styled hotel, restaurant and bar. It is quite elegant and has exquisite oriental gardens and decor. Many Hollywood movies which called for authentic Japanese scenes were shot there, such as *Sayonara*, which starred Marlon Brando.

The Roy Porter Sounds, which featured Tollie Moore on keyboards, Maurice Simon on tenor sax and flute and Chuck Norris on guitar, stayed at the Yamashiro for over a year playing music on Friday and Saturday nights for dinner and dancing. Generally we played ballads and dinner music during the meal time. Then at 10 p.m., when the younger people began arriving, we'd play jazz and some rock.

In early 1971 we left the Yamashiro and opened at a joint called the Swing, located out on Ventura Boulevard in Studio City. The Swing was just about what the name implied, but it was about two weeks before I actually got hip to what was happening out there. The place catered to those who wanted to swap spouses. Our quartet was able to stretch out musically, but it was a bit of a drag since all they wanted was rock and roll, nothing else. We lasted four weeks there and then I had to move on.

On my next gig I worked about six weeks with Teddy Edwards at the Tiki Club on 36th and Western. That band was really scalding, with Teddy, Cat Anderson, Thurman Green, Leroy Vinnegar, Billy Mitchell and me. It's just too bad that the group was never recorded.

It was a little lean for a time there, but then I got a call from bassist Johnny Parker to play the Holiday Inn Hotel up in California City, which is a desert resort community near Lancaster. That job lasted six weeks and was nice for the change of atmosphere. During the day you could fish or swim, but it was always so damn hot. On my days off I could drive back to Los Angeles and take Daryl my son back with me. Daryl could ride his mini-bike to his heart's content out there in the desert.

By this time I was divorced. This happened in 1968, when Tina divorced me for mental cruelty. This was due to my incessant alcohol and drug abuse and I didn't even blame her when it came about. At that point, I was too far gone to realize what was happening, but we have remained good friends since then. I don't think that Tina has been so good about this just because of our Daryl or because we were in business together with Rotine Music. She is just a beautiful woman.

When I was up in California City I was not drinking and I was really starting to feel pretty good. Maybe it was because I was out and way from the big city. But as soon as we closed and I returned to Los Angeles I went on a binge for a whole month. What triggered this behavior I do not know. I was drinking and dropping amphetamines pretty heavily and it finally just took its toll. It got so bad that my lady friend then, Jessica, took me out to Synanon.

I went into Synanon on a Friday morning and left the following Sunday evening, so I was there a little over 48 hours. The first thing I know I'm in a barber's chair and this dude is cutting off all my hair. Next they are giving me some clothes to wear as a sort of Synanon uniform. Then I found myself sitting up in a room with a bunch of people in a so-called rap session. This was part of the Synanon games. Basically, the rap session boiled down to being locked up in a room where other people verbally took their hostilities out on one another. These sessions were a daily requirement and they believed that this was a type of psychological therapy.

I still hadn't seen any medication. Next, after you're more or less stunned from all of the hostilities from the rap session, you are led into one of Chuck Diedrich's hench-man's offices. There they are talking shit to you and really putting the bite on you to turn over all of your property to the Synanon Foundation. So I got real tired of all of these intimidating tactics and said, the hell with this, I can do this at home. I asked to leave, but the Synanon authorities put up such strong resistance that I had to come up with another plan. I borrowed a dime and called my friend Jessica, told her to come and pick me up six blocks away and then walked out.

The Synanon methods were supposed to be humbling, and were supposed to bring about a different attitude. But about all I got out of the deal was a bald head. I had to wear a cap on my gigs for quite a while after that. I learned a bit more about life and myself from my stay in Synanon, but just about everyone whom I have spoken with has since pointed out that the Synanon Foundation has been in trouble with the various communities where their institutions have been located.

I wound up at Synanon more or less by default. I had been out to the Veteran Administration Hospital, drug and alcohol rehabilitation facilities, and was refused admission because there was no bed space. I was told to go home and wait and that they would admit me as soon as a bed was available. Hell, I needed help right then. Jessica called Synanon and they said to come out right away. I went, but reluctantly, because I'd heard about the Synanon "games." I didn't know about the hair-cutting and the no-smoking policy. Neither did I know that you couldn't get any kind of medication to help you make it during the first few days.

From other accounts of this time period, 1971, I understand that Art Pepper and Esther Phillips were in that same facility in Venice then, but I didn't see either of them during my stay. I know that Stan Kenton became a Synanon resident and later died in a Synanon house. I did see Stymie Beard, whom I had known for years from the streets in Los Angeles. Stymie used to be in the old "Our Gang" or "Little Rascals" movies. Stymie was actually a permanent Synanon resident and had been playing the games for years. In fact both he and Art Pepper later married Synanon games

women. Stymie was into Synanon so much that he actually
tried to talk me into staying. This would have been a real
feather in his game cap. A few years later I'd see Stymie in
the Page Four bar, drinking booze right along with me. I
asked him what happened after all those years at Synanon.
He kind of smiled and said, "You know Roy, all games have
to play out sometime."

After I rested up at home for a while and was feeling
better, Bumps Blackwell shows up saying, "It's about time
for you to record an album of your own. Think it over." I
started rehearsing three horn players and five rhythm men
for an album. Most of the musicians were not well known.
The exceptions were Tollie Moore Jr on keyboards, Jack
Fulks on tenor sax and flute and Lester Robertson on
trombone. I made sure that each individual could contribute
an arrangement of their own originals. Since most of the
musicians were young, I didn't have any real problems with
ego trips or any scenes. The album we recorded was entitled
Jessica and the remaining personnel included Charles Jones,
bass; Oscar Dye, congas; Bob Davis, organ; Hense Powell,
flugelhorn; and Jimmy Holloway (Red Holloway's son),
guitar.

Jessica was recorded in 1971 at an eight-track studio on
Adams. The title track was written for my lady friend. I
wasn't satisfied with the album's sound, but with the
assistance of Bumps we put together a credible effort. It was
released later in 1971 and made a bit of noise locally. All-jazz
KBCA played the LP locally a bit and the more pop-oriented
KJLH had another cut from the album, a Jack Fulks
composition, *Hip City*, on their playlist for quite some time. I
have to give the credit for *Hip City* getting over like it did to
KJLH DJ Doug Moore. He really pushed it and played that
track all the time.

We put a rather unusual tune on that album that was a lot
of fun to record. It was called *Drums for Daryl*, and was
named for my son. Back then Daryl was very involved with
moto-cross motorcycle racing (and had been fascinated with
motorbikes and motorcycles since he was ten). I had a tape

that I had recorded in 1959 with a Nigerian master conga drummer named Louis Polieman Brown. It was just me on my drums and Louis on congas and it was pretty far out, with a lot of polyrhythms and great call-and-response things – nothing but drums for ten minutes. So, on top of this Bumps and I layered in a tape of motorcycle and dune-buggy sounds which we had made out at the Indian Dunes moto-cross raceway. In addition Bumps brought in Arne Frager and Jamie Wilson on synthesizers to give it a rather ethereal sound. It took two engineers three days to get it to where Bumps was satisfied, but Bumps, to his credit, knew exactly what he wanted. There was some debate about whether we should include *Drums for Daryl* in the album since it was obviously not a very commercial piece. But I decided to include it anyway, since we had put so much into it at that point.

Drums would have made a great soundtrack for a sports picture. In fact, we had been in touch with Steve McQueen's people about it since he was a big motorcycle race fan. This didn't ever get off the ground, though, and later, when I was thinking of re-submitting it, he died of cancer.

All things considered, *Jessica* had some great moments and it was personally rewarding for me to record the Sound Machine band. Again, all of the faith that Bumps had in me and all of the time that he personally put into the project were a real source of pride.

I was still fighting my migraine headaches with prescribed medication and booze. I still saw Dr Kim occasionally, since he had moved his offices from Jefferson to Crenshaw Boulevard. It wasn't regular like it had been from 1957 through 1969, though, and then I started going to Martin Luther King Hospital. Nothing seemed to work for me and I kept right on with my heavy drinking. I've been busted so many times for drunk driving that I should damn near own city hall by now. I had it down to a science when it came to drinking and driving. Luckily I've been fortunate about accidents.

In Los Angeles I know just about every bar, beer joint or

other establishment that sold booze before or after hours. I learned a lot of alleyways and off the beaten streets just so I could lose the police when they were on my tail. If I saw the cops and I thought they were following me I'd pull over, park the car, get out and knock on anyone's door as if I'd reached my destination. It didn't make any difference to me what time of day or night it was, as long as I was not behind the wheel if they stopped me. Sometimes that hustle didn't work and the cops would take me down to jail.

Alcohol has been a real demon to me. I had to leave it alone because I was coming close to insanity and death with it. That old saying "A drunk ain't shit" is true. You'll lie and connive, won't bathe or otherwise take care of yourself, and always find a way to get that next drink. When I see all of the homeless and hungry, destitute tent people, I just think, "There but for the grace of God go I." That sight always makes me pause and think about my life. Most of all I am thankful to a higher power that I've been able to take my drinking problem one day at a time and have been sober since 1981.

During the 1970s I was able to work many gigs with the Sound Machine. Even though they were mostly unknown, all of the band members enjoyed working together. We played at dinner houses, nightclubs and a lot of private parties for dancing. We played just about everything, from jazz, to rock, to R & B to MOR. We gave the people what they wanted to hear, including James Brown, Blood, Sweat and Tears, Aretha Franklin, Creedence Clearwater Revival and even Guy Lombardo.

In 1975 I took a chance and made another album with the Sound Machine, *Inner Feelings*. We recorded it during three months at Spectrum Studios in Venice. It was recorded on an eight-track machine and came out fairly well. This was a gamble, but I have always been a gambler when it comes to music. It was a decent album, but it never really got the airplay on radio which it needed and so it didn't make much noise locally or nationally. The airplay the *Inner Feelings* LP did receive was through the efforts of Carole King, a very tenancious A & R and promotion person. Carole later joined Casablanca Records, working with Donna Summer.

Being a believer in that old adage "You are born a person, but you make yourself a personality," over the years I had knocked on many doors of record companies and personal managers. I was told again and again that my songs, and even *Lonesome Mood*, didn't fit the format of the day. Total jive. Sure the music was modern. But it was published by my own company and most of the record industry frowns on independent people. If I had given up the publishing rights to my music, I'm sure that things would have been different.

In this mid-70s period my career as a working drummer took a back seat to my work as a composer. I was proud of *Lonesome Mood*, and when the Friends of Distinction made that a hit in 1969 I wanted to duplicate that success. I was still working gigs and doing some recording but my heart was not in my playing. Whether this was the right decision or not is hard to say in retrospect. But all of my writing activity did broaden my knowledge of music, especially thanks to my understanding of the piano keyboard. Still, during this time I had bouts of severe depression, and with the migraines, medication and alcohol I was depressed more and more.

In 1976 Patricia Willard was sent to my home to get information from me on behalf of Savoy Records, who were bringing out material by my big band from the late 1940s. I had known Patricia since those days when she was a journalism major at Los Angeles City College. (Eric Dolphy was a student at LACC during that same time.) Pat came by a couple of concerts of my big band and she was certainly a dedicated and true-blue bebop fan.

She used to catch the streetcar regularly from her apartment in Hollywood near Melrose and come to the east side to be on the Central Avenue scene. She was also working for disc jockey Gene Norman on radio station KFWB, which featured a good mixture of bebop records.

However, when Pat came by my house for her interview I was caught very much unawares. This was all out of the blue, since no one from Savoy, such as Bob Porter who was producing this reissue package, called *Black California*, had even bothered to contact me, let alone get me a royalty contract. So when the telephone rang and then Pat later interviewed me I was apprehensive. I assumed that she was in on this rather shabby business practice and knew exactly what Bob Porter was doing. Poor Pat really was stuck in the middle of a messy situation. She had only been hired to write the liner notes for the album. But I didn't learn this until much later, when Pat claimed that she, too, had been taken advantage of.

At any rate, when I finally talked to Bob Porter on the phone, he tells me in a rather high-handed manner that whether I like it or not the album is going to be released and, in fact, "It is just about ready to go out now." He then promised me a royalty contract. To this day I haven't seen a royalty or any other type of contract from Savoy Records. In order to get any payment I had to call Clive Davis at Arista Records, who were distributing the *Black California* LP. To Davis's credit, he promptly sent out a contract and a check.

In my opinion, Bob Porter showed a total disrespect for all of the artists on the project and especially to me. But Porter is just one in a long line of jazz record company executives who really care very little for the artists who produce this music. He epitomizes this cavalier attitude that has rarely tried to help black musicians and for the most part has bled us dry.

For years I tried to purchase the masters of my 1949 recording session from Herman Lubinsky at Savoy Records, but was refused. Then, when they decide to put the material out 29 years later, in 1978, they have some fast talker like Bob Porter who creates a good deal of animosity with his egotistical and heavy-handed work methods. In fact, I heard from others who were involved in this project that they never received a cent for any royalties. Even though I was pleased that this material did get released, I was nonetheless shocked that musicians were still being treated in a second-class manner.

All the while the 1970s were turning into the most turbulent years of my life because of alcohol and pills. When

Dr Kim had warned me in 1957 that if I kept on with my drinking I'd turn into an alcoholic, I should have heeded his words. The juice was slowly taking its toll. My life was filled with guilt, shame, unfulfillment, and a paranoia that only a person who has been an alcoholic and drug abuser can comprehend. Bars, beer joints and the streets became my existence when I was not gigging or recording. My work started slipping away, of course, as my condition got worse. It seemed like I was in and out of jail a ridiculous amount of time due to drunk driving. In 1973 I had three drunk driving convictions in two months. For that maneuver my driver's license was snatched from me for five years. No sweat. I got another Social Security number and a driver's license in another name from another state and kept right on with this insanity. Six months later I had accumulated three more DUI's (Driving Under the Influence), and so I had to junk that license too. But I drove anyway.

I've been robbed, beaten, and in fights all because of alcohol. The police had stopped me so many times that they knew who I was. Had they not recognized me one time when they stopped me, and frisked me, they would have found a gun in my pocket. Once I was being robbed by two dudes and since I had this piece I could have blown them away, but didn't. Insanity had definitely taken over, but there must have been a higher power watching over me because I never used the gun.

One of the stupidest things I've ever done was to slap the police officer who was fingerprinting me in the station one of the many times I was thrown into jail. There's the saying "the devil made me do it." Well, the alcohol and pills made me do that. Three cops beat me, knocked me down and kicked me, fracturing two ribs. Then they threw me into an isolated cell for two days. I was lucky because they could just as easily have killed me and nothing would have been done about it. I had to go to the hospital after being released, but since I'd been booked under an alias I didn't have any legal leg to stand on.

In any given situation there always seems to be a crisis that can turn a situation round, if you have the knowledge to recognize it. For a week straight I had been drinking right along with my medication, Cafergot tablets for migraines and Valium for my nerves. On 14 February 1976 I had gone to bed drunk as usual. About 2.30 a.m. I woke up with a headache that felt like I'd been shot in the head by a 12-gauge shotgun. When I opened my eyes I couldn't see anything. For about 30 seconds I panicked, but slowly a glimmer of light came to me. Still, my peripheral vision in both eyes was gone. I didn't know what to do except lie there and try to figure out whether this was going to be permanent.

When I got to the hospital the doctors couldn't figure out why a headache could cause that kind of damage to my eyes. It wasn't until six months later that they decided that the medication which they had prescribed for me along with all of the alcohol had helped to bring about the stroke. I was transferred from Martin Luther King Hospital to the Veterans Administration, Wadsworth Hospital. There they determined that the Cafergot, which is one of the strongest drugs prescribed for migraines, along with the Valium which I abused, prescribed by the doctors from Martin Luther King, had helped to induce my stroke. The doctors at the VA told me that this reaction was a rarity. For my part, I found that the left side of my body became weaker than my right. This malady persists, and when I am stepping up or down from a curb, frequently I'll stumble or stagger.

It took the doctors six months to finally find out that I had just suffered from a major stroke. That headache hit with such force that the blood vessels in back of my eyes burst and bled, destroying my peripheral vision. This is something that I live with, although I am very thankful that I have any eyesight at all.

After resting up I retained enough of my faculties so that I could work whatever gigs or record dates came my way. Also in this period of acute depression I feel that I composed some of my best songs, tunes which have yet to be heard.

Despite all of this madness I was able to evaluate my

situation and decided to face up to the fact that I was my own worst enemy. I knew that I was the one that had put myself into each and every position that caused terrible things to happen to me. I presume that is why some of my sanity was spared. While it seemed that I might have been getting better, this was not the case.

When I was in the care unit of the Hospital for Alcohol and Drug Abuse I had to attend Alcoholics Anonymous meetings regularly. AA has its good and bad points. Its philosophy allows alcoholics to draw strength from each other's experiences. But I feel that deep down you have to use your own strength to overcome your personal weaknesses yourself. Still, if I feel as if I am going to be weak and am thinking about drinking, I'll read *One Day at a Time*. This book will usually wake me up and bring back all the memories of how it was before, and then I'll lose my cravings. When I feel that it's necessary, then I attend the AA meetings – every day if need be.

But even after all of this healthy philosophy I didn't get any better. After being in the hospital that first time in 1981 I went right back out and did the same thing. Nothing stopped me. I heard of my colleagues dying from drugs, alcohol and rumored suicides, but nothing slowed me down. Friends tried to reason with me. Loved ones pleaded. Doctors counseled and advised. They even had me detoxified in the care unit that first time, but that didn't work out either. But the second time I wound up in the hospital something changed.

I had only been out of the hospital for one day and I was gone again. During that week I blacked out. I fell down at home and couldn't get up off the floor to use the telephone for over three hours. But when I did manage to get back up I was gone again. I wrecked my car and received another DUI ticket and went to jail. Yet during this entire week I cannot remember anything. It was a total blackout. To this day I can't recall what happened during that week. That was the crisis that made me want to live.

When they took me to the hospital the second time in 1981

The big band at the Avadon Ballroom, 1949 (above, left to right): Paul Sparks (vocals), Wayne Harris (bass), Kenny Bright, Reuben McFall (trumpets), Danny Horton (trombone), William "Boogie" Daniels, Teddy Edwards, Bob Gordon (saxophones), Roy (directing); (below) Wayne Harris (bass), Jimmy Pratt (bongos), Roy (drums), Kenny Bright, Reuben McFall, Art Farmer (trumpets), Danny Horton, John Pettigrew (trombones), Charles René (congas), William "Boogie" Daniels, Wilbur Brown, René Bloch, Teddy Edwards, Bob Gordon (saxophones), Paul Sparks (vocals)

The big band at the Lincoln Theater, Los Angeles, 1949 (left to right): Robert Ross (trumpet), Eric Dolphy (alto saxophone), Wilbur Brown (alto saxophone), Hadley Caliman (tenor saxophone), Roy (drums), Cylde Dunn (baritone saxophone), Damita Jo (vocals)

The wreck of the car in which Roy, Art Farmer and Clyde Dunn were traveling, Deming, New Mexico, 1949

At Bop City, San Francisco, 1951 (back, left to right): George Walker, Eddie ?, Atlee Chapman, Roy, Dexter Gordon, Jimmy Heath, Chuck Thompson (seated at drums), Joe Stone (bass), Percy Heath, Howard Jeffries, Milt Jackson (at piano), Sonny Criss, Jimbo Edwards (center), Hampton Hawes (seated, center front)

Bop City, 1951 (left to right): Dexter Gordon, Jimmy Heath, Atlee Chapman, Eric Miller, Roy, Milt Jackson, Percy Heath, Hampton Hawes, Howard Jeffries, Joe Stone, Chuck Thompson, Sonny Criss, Jimbo Edwards

More at Bop City, c1951 (back, left to right): Roy, Specs Wright, Bernie Peters, Jimbo Edwards, Pat ?, Betty Bennett, Kenny Dorham, Dizzy Gillespie, Miles Davis, Howard Jeffries, Percy Heath; (front) Ernie Lewis, Sonny Criss, Milt Jackson, Carl Perkins, Jimmy Heath, Henry "Cowboy" Noyd, Oyama Johnson

Vernon Alley's quartet at the Blackhawk, San Francisco, c1951: Richard Wyands (piano), Pony Poindexter (also saxophone), Roy (drums), Vernon Alley (bass)

Tina Collins, Las Vegas, 1957   *Roy at Bop City, 1952*

Maurice Simon, Billie Holiday and Freddie Simon (foreground) at Billy Berg's Waldorf Cellar, Los Angeles, 1952

Eric Dolphy and Lawrence Marable (seated, far right) with unknown musicians at a jam session at the Club Oasis, Los Angeles, 1956–7

The dancers with Eric Dolphy's band at the Club Oasis, 1956 (left to right): Flo ?, Frances Neely, Donna Jones and Sylvia Moon

Roy at the Hacienda Hotel, 1965–6

Donna Jean Gentry, Club Oasis, Los Angeles, 1955

Eddie Preston, 1980s

Red Callender, 1947

Sallie Blair, 1966

Clora Bryant, Rag Doll Club, Los Angeles, 1957

Horace Tapscott, 1980s

Jimmy Knepper, 1980s

Members of the Roy Porter Sound Machine at Spectrum Recording Studios, Venice, CA, c1975 (from the top): Arne Frager, Roy, Roy Thompson, Randy Pigge, Hugh Bell, Tollie Moore Jr, Charlemagne Payne, Charles Jones, Hense Powell, Wallace Huff

Roy Porter Sounds, Mr Woodley's Club, Los Angeles, 1969: Tollie Moore Jr, Ray Brookis and Roy

Roy with Henry Smith of Knockout and Debonair Records, 1985

my mind was made up. I had had enough. That was the last time I had a drink and I haven't abused any pills since that time either. As I've said, because I am an alcoholic and realize this, I belong to AA and attend their meetings intermittently. When I feel the need for spiritual and moral guidance these meetings are a tremendous source of strength. They provide you with encouragement, but in the end the individual is the one who has to leave the chemicals alone.

Meanwhile all around me my friends and fellow professionals in the music world were dropping like flies. Giants such as Sonny Criss, Gene Ammons, John Coltrane, Paul Gonsalves, Frank Butler, Sonny Stitt, Paul Sparks, Benny White and many more are dead. In addition to the famous ones, those others mentioned were members of the Roy Porter Big Band. And while not all of their deaths were directly attributed to alcohol or drug abuse, many of them were. Years earlier, Big Sid Catlett and one of the all-time great jazz drummers, Shadow Wilson, who was a user, had both left us. More recently, Tollie Moore Jr, who played piano with my Sound Machine group, and Robert "Bumps" Blackwell, the kind and charitable soul who taught me so much about producing and the business of music, have gone too.

All of these deaths have forced me to evaluate my own position in the music world. I know I was a damn good drummer, but I would really like to be remembered as a composer. Still, I suppose my position as the "archetypal bebop drummer" will be forever secured thanks to my work on that Dial session with Charlie Parker in 1946. After that I became known as the "bomb dropper."

A "bomb" is an accented beat with the left hand on the snare drum and your foot on the bass drum. Done correctly this produces a "tee-boom" sound. I took this style one step further and made the sound by using the snare drum, tom toms and bass drum simultaneously. This will give a "brrr-oom" exploding sound. My bombs exploded the way I played them. No other drummer was getting that sound then. On many occasions critics would scratch their heads and say, "What is he doing back there, slamming doors?" They just didn't have a clue. Time has moved on.

I am not sure about all of the reasons which I gave myself on why I did not seriously study music. Perhaps it was laziness because I never enjoyed practicing, so I never practiced. Since I had a scholarship to study journalism at college, my experience was somewhat different, but I have always felt that many black musicians have not gone on to formally study music and receive that training which is essential for certain types of success because of simple economics. Most black parents did not have the finances to give their children private lessons, tutors, private teachers or the best musical schools. This, of course, continues to this day. Nevertheless, I believe that where there is a will there is a way and one's destiny is left up to the individual. I was fortunate because the drummers of my era were not required to possess so much formal training. If they had good ears and knew their instrument they could generally get over. Not so today.

8

The Present

In retrospect I have had a fortunate, lucky, and even blessed life. And while I have had my share of bad times, there have also been a number of good things that have happened to me. It seems that I have always had many people around me that have been in my corner and have encouraged me in my various endeavors, whatever I attempted to do. These friends have made me into a very rich human being. I don't mean this strictly from an economic point of view, but rather spiritually, mentally and even psychically. Material objects have never been a top priority with me, but they have more or less fallen into my lap.

But far more important to me are those friends that I have. I have always told these people that just because they don't hear from me that often, it doesn't mean that I don't think of them and do not love them. I love people, but there are just some that I can tolerate and others that I can only take in small doses.

I see some hope in the youth of today, because many of them are seekers and will listen and try to learn about our past. After all, the youth of today are our future. And without the past there can be no future, because there is no foundation – nothing to build on. Today's youth have taken music into a number of other directions, but they have to stay aware of their roots and recall the people that have laid the groundwork and given them something to build on. Of these young musicians, I respect some of their playing, but only tolerate some of their attitudes. Respect is not given, it is earned. At the beginning of the bebop scene there seemed to be less ego trips, since most musicians were trying to develop their playing and were really searching to find common paths and ways to work together. Today, in many cases, I see all too many ego trips. What saddens me the most is that so many young black musicians have forgotten and even forsaken jazz, their musical heritage, for the easy, commercial out of funk music. This is a pity. In point of fact, if it were not for some white people, college students, Europeans, the Japanese, and the middle-aged people of all races who came up with this music and have not forgotten it, I am afraid that this music would have totally fallen by the wayside. As it is, jazz is a lot like classical music. It has its loyal, true blue fans, but they are a distinct minority.

In terms of my life in jazz, I consider it a great honor to have been the drummer on Charlie Parker's first and second Dial recording sessions. *Night in Tunisia*, *Yardbird Suite*, *Moose the Mooche* and *Ornithology* are all classics. What might be hard for some fans to understand, since this music has become so accepted in jazz circles, is that when these records were being made none of us knew exactly where Bird was going with his ideas. All the musicians on those sessions were searching on their instruments. I know I sure was. The only cat who wasn't was Bird himself. Charlie Parker always knew exactly where he was going with his music, if not his life.

Another first and a most satisfying experience for me was my big band which I led from 1948 through 1950. Most of the time I was working with this band I'd be having thoughts like, "Damn, Roy. Do you realize what you have here? All this big sound around you?" But, fool that I was, I wasn't able to act on this realization at that time. I didn't really grasp that the band was one of the best in the country for that idiom and that it was the *only* 17-piece bebop big band ever organized by a drummer on the West Coast. And even though it took almost 30 years, those recordings that the big band made for Savoy Records were eventually released and helped make a lot of people aware of the wonderful music that we were making then.

In terms of the pioneers, the innovators of this music, many of them whom I dearly loved have been taken away from us. Fats Navarro was one of the first. Only a partial list includes Bud Powell, Kenny Dorham, Charlie Parker, Wardell Gray, Shifty Henry, Sonny Criss, Charles Mingus and Hampton Hawes. From my big band there was Eric Dolphy, Leroy "Sweetpea" Robinson, Joe Stone, Robert Ross, Wiggie Wiginton, Joe Howard, Addison Farmer and Joe Harrison. All of these greats, plus innumerable others who have all gone, really make me take stock and wonder how I have managed to still be here.

Mentioning Hamp reminds me of one of the last times I saw him. He had just gotten home from the federal penitentiary for narcotics violations and came by my house to pick up a lead sheet and tape of *Lonesome Mood*. Hamp was in good spirits and we had a long discussion about the pros and cons of publishing one's own music. After this he began telling me about a girl he had met while in Japan that he thought was going to be a great pianist and arranger. Her name was Toshiko Akiyoshi. Hamp went into great detail how she used to sit up under him every night and learn everything she could from him. Now, of course, she's been in the United States for many years and is a respected member of the jazz scene, but Hampton Hawes taught her a lot.

The last time I saw Hamp was not so pleasant. Along with Dolo Coker, Teddy Edwards, Louis Lodge and Oscar Brashear, I was playing at the Lighthouse in Redondo Beach. Hamp came in and sat at the bar. During intermission I tried to talk with him but it was very painful because I knew just from looking at him that he was seriously ill. Not so long after this, he was dead.

Another great whom I'll never forget was Sonny Criss. Sonny was an entirely different breed of individual. As I recall, Sonny lived in Watts, on Mary Street off 103rd, with a family of means. His mother, Mrs Lucy Criss, was behind his career 100 per cent, almost to the point of worship. Mrs Criss owned a women's fashion shop on Western Avenue and made a good living with this business. Consequently Sonny had a fine music rehearsal room, beautiful Mercedes automobiles and the finances to back it up. All of this made Sonny into a very independent person. I generally got along with Sonny, whom I deeply admired, but all of his independence was sometimes misunderstood by his peers. We were close, and in later years we often talked of our mutual problem, alcohol. Sonny died in 1977, but I did not know until recently that he was a victim of cancer.

More recently we've lost two of the real inspirations in jazz drumming, Mr Papa Jo Jones and Philly Joe Jones. Papa Jo was not only a first-class player, but he was also a great contributor to a highly developed art form. His death saddens me greatly. Aside from a few small items in the jazz press, I haven't seen or heard much in the media about their deaths. But you know that if it had been some jive rock and roller of the same stature there would be headlines, special bulletins and all that.

On the brighter side, that same year, 1977, KPFK-FM radio personality John Breckow presented a jazz concert called "Groovin' High" in Baxter Lecture Hall at California Technical Institute in Pasadena. It was a soulful group featuring Joe Albany on piano, Harry Babasin on bass, Sahib Shihab on alto and baritone saxophones, Art Pepper on alto sax and me on drums. It was a cooking concert and was the last time that I saw Art Pepper alive, a rather forceful reminder that you never really know what dues a person is paying even when you work with them. We played some classic bop, with songs like *Groovin' High*, *Night in Tunisia* and *Ornithology*. On that last one Art and Sahib traded chorus after chorus, then they broke it down to eight bars, and then four, and finally two bars. At that point Joe, Harry and I each took a chorus. The crowd was small but enthusiastic and I enjoyed this concert because I hadn't played a jazz concert in quite a while.

These days I can't help reflecting on the plight of the black musician. Whether the field is blues, R & B, rock and roll or jazz, our ideas have been imitated, stolen and capitalized on. Historically, the early blues guitarists and singers were taken out of the cotton fields and put into a jive-ass studio. After they had recorded their originals someone else became the writer of the song and the black artist received nothing for his creation.

When race records and later rhythm-and-blues records became popular in the 1940s and 50s, black musicians were still taken into funky studios and recorded with very little preparation or rehearsal of the material. If the record started selling, the musician was given maybe a couple of hundred dollars and enough money for a down payment on a Cadillac. Most black artists were not even aware of proper contracts, copyrights or publishing, and so by and large they were routinely taken. I have personally made jazz, rhythm-and-blues and rock-and-roll records with name musicians and have watched them receive next to nothing compared with what their records sold. Most of the time this happens because the musician did not take care of business.

In my experience most managers, booking agents and accountants (black or white) will steal from their clients if they can. This is especially true of uneducated black artists who know nothing of their own business affairs. For openers there was Fats Domino. Fats lost a lot. Of course, this happens to everyone, but it seems to happen most frequently with black artists. Another classic example is Charlie Parker. Though he died a pauper, the record companies that recorded him are still making money off of his records. Little Richard is going through the same thing right now, trying to get what is owed to him. I believe that most of these artists did not take the time to research their business dealings, since they hoped that they were on their way to being accepted into the mainstream of white society. So on we trod. Even today, many black musicians find it hard to realize that we are a mainstream.

At the artistic level, ideas were also appropriated. Many times I have seen white musicians come into a club when black musicians were playing bebop. Their only purpose was to learn everything about black jazz. Of these white musicians there were only a few, like Jimmy Knepper and Barney Kessel, who learned a lot from Charlie Christian in

Oklahoma, and a very few others, that really made the grade around here and were able to musically keep up with us. Whether this was because of the feeling, chord changes in the tunes themselves, or tempos or meter, I've never been sure. I've even had drummers sit up under me and listen to me and take certain ideas of mine, all the while telling me how much they dig my playing. Then the next time I see them elsewhere they hardly wanted to speak. Next thing I know I'm listening to one of their records and they are playing four or eight bars of my stuff. Sometimes they would bring their girlfriends or wives around to the set or even to my home to visit, play records, get high, or talk about bebop music and get into your mind, all the while knowing that the chick is going to have eyes for me. I finally got enough fat on my head and brought that shit to a halt by playing less when I saw their faces come through the door.

All kinds of things were happening then, but even today there still is not much toleration for a black man to be seen with a white woman. Some will tolerate it, others not. During those days it was not uncommon to meet white women at clubs in Hollywood, who would come to the east side, spend time with you under the covers, then later, if you'd happen to see her again in Hollywood, she didn't know you. These same women, when they got angry with you, the first thing they would call you was a nigger.

On the other side of the coin there were many black musicians who were happy to have white women or musicians come around and be on the scene. The musicians would sit in at the jam sessions on Central Avenue. This made the black musicians feel that they were being accepted into the mainstream of an alienated society which mostly rejected Blacks. Even some of the most intelligent black men succumbed to this white-woman syndrome, ending up with any woman that came along just so they could say that they had a white woman. Very few black musicians whom I've known have had their musical careers enhanced by this type of association.

By the same token I don't have much time for black

women who harbor the same attitude toward white men. You can believe this behavior exists if an elephant is heavy.

In another department, I have been asked why I have not received the recognition which I deserve and, specifically, why I was not included in certain jazz reference works. I have found that all through history that pioneers, inventors and innovators have usually been the last to receive credit for their accomplishments. After recording with Charlie Parker here in Los Angeles I was given recognition all over the world. In 1946 and 1947 I was listed in the *Down Beat* and *Metronome* polls for drummers. But I have probably not been as visible as others in the jazz world. When I had my big band from 1948 through 1950, an automobile accident cut short what could have been an extensive chapter in my musical career. My incarceration from 1953 to 1956 further took me off the scene. But, truthfully, after getting out of prison I became more interested in composing than playing drums. Maybe if I had been more of the grinning, head-scratching, hang-out type of person things might have been a little different, but I doubt it.

In terms of proper recognition, both financial and otherwise, while Charlie Parker was well known at the time of his death, he died a pauper. The list of those who were never really recognized by the critics or the public is a long one, but some of those that come to mind include Sonny Criss, Hampton Hawes, Carl Perkins, Frank Butler and Wardell Gray. Many of the true giants of this music, even if they did receive some degree of public recognition, went out of this world penniless.

I find some degree of hope, nevertheless, in the reissue programs of some of the record companies today. These projects are certainly getting the music out to an audience. As mentioned, the *Black California* album provided people with an aural glimpse of what our big band was doing in the late 1940s. Another recent reissue from Savoy Records which contains a good slice of musical history from this time is *The Hunt*, which was recorded at the great jam session on 6 July 1947 at the old Elks Hall on Central Avenue. The producer of this reissue, Bob Porter, lists Connie Kay as the drummer on this jam, but Connie didn't even come to California until years later, when he traveled out here with the Modern Jazz Quartet. Neither does he play or sound at all like me.

All of this leads me to the old adage "Look out for your own." That is, instead of just complaining about the situation, *do* something about it. There are certainly enough black people within the music industry that have the qualifications, skills and money to begin to change this situation, yet we still have to get rid of the mental slavery attitude and get our heads out of the sand. There won't be much change until we have more black writers and critics that care about jazz. We also need a lot more black musicians that are proud of their jazz heritage. We need dedicated black-owned jazz record companies, commercial jazz radio stations and, most importantly, an audience that will support, not forsake, their music.

On the other hand there has been real progress made. In the years 1945–7 it was routine for the swing or dixieland players to put the bebop cats down. There was an incident at the Jade Palace then when Howard McGhee's band was alternating sets with Kid Ory. At one point Ory became so enraged at this music that he refused to play any more and stalked out of the club. I guess he thought that his fans would leave the club when his band left. But he had no such luck. The people stayed, and that club stayed packed for another four to six weeks with people who were checking out pure, undiluted bebop.

In other cities, Louis Armstrong, bless his soul, was putting Dizzy Gillespie and the rest of the bebop players down. Cab Calloway did the same thing, and I never did know whether Cab even played an instrument. There are, of course, many others, but it's no use to call names. It even took the studio musicians quite a while to accept this new art form.

At this same time, circa 1945, Scatman Crothers was playing opposite Howard McGhee's band at the Swing Club on Hollywood Boulevard. But it didn't make any difference to him. Maggie's band would play bebop and then Scat's band would play swing, leaning towards bebop. With cats in his band like Benny Bailey on trumpet, Vic McMillan on bass and Will Smith on alto, those guys could play both kinds of music. Scatman was also quite an innovator, and in addition to being one of the first and best scat singers, he was one hell of a drummer. On top of that he could play most of the string instruments, such as guitar, ukelele, and tiple, and was one of the greatest showmen in the business.

Many of the blues players never really understood bebop music either. And some of them didn't know their instruments well enough to play anything more complex than blues changes. Still, most everyone got along pretty well, at least on the surface.

It took the film industry years before it accepted bebop jazz scores. When it did begin to start using this music it came from people like Gerald Wilson, Quincy Jones, Lalo Schifrin (who got his start playing piano with Dizzy Gillespie) and Benny Carter. The gut-level bebop player is responsible for giving these people the tools to work with. Today, most all of your movies and television utilize some jazz elements in their scores.

A variety of radio stations serving Southern California have had an influence on my life. I'll begin by thanking all of the disc jockeys. Many of them helped make my name known as a composer. Not only did they play the hell out of *Lonesome Mood*, but then they went on to inform the audience that a local drummer, Roy Porter, was the composer of this hit song. And since my full name was not even printed on the album jacket or record itself, this was a very helpful thing for my career and turned a lot of people on to my music and to my writing skills.

In the 1940s jazz was played for the Los Angeles audience by a few pioneers. When bebop was moving out of the ghetto and into Hollywood and other parts of town, a white disc jockey, Gene Norman, played quite a bit of good music on KFWB. This was an AM radio station (as they all were then) which had a powerful signal and was one of the biggest in the city. Norman, who went on to make a name for himself with concert promotion and with his own record label, played a lot of Charlie Parker's songs. He also featured Howard McGhee's band on live broadcasts from KFWB and played a lot of Dexter Gordon and Wardell. Tunes like *The Chase, Jeronimo* and *Blues in Teddy's Flat*, the latter with Teddy Edwards, all received substantial airplay. I was on those records, and it was always a kick hearing yourself on the radio. Gene later went on to run a nightclub on Sunset Boulevard called The Crescendo, which always featured a lot of name jazz musicians. I remember one great night when I caught Basie's band there when the place was packed and Basie was sounding very strong.

Another disc jockey who didn't do much for bebop but did play a lot of this music during the early days was Al Jarvis at KLAC. He'd play pop material and big-band swing, everything from Horace Heidt and Wayne King to Tommy Dorsey. Al's program, "Make Believe Ballroom," was very popular with listeners here.

After Savoy Records recorded my big band in 1948, disc jockeys like Bill Sampson of KWKW, Hunter Hancock at KRKD, Charles Trammel on KGFJ (who broadcast from Dolphins Record Store at Vernon and Central) and Roy Loggins on KALI all played my records. They'd play my records even though at that time none of these guys were considered to be bebop jocks. They mostly played race records and other rhythm-and-blues type of material, but they must have figured that I crossed over because they played my records with the big band.

Joe Adams worked for KOWL in Santa Monica, where he played more established cats like Count Basie, although he did spin my records a couple of times. He surely liked my vocalist, Damita Jo, though, since he'd frequently come by our shows just to catch her. He was the one who talked Damita into leaving the band.

Hunter Hancock was one of the few white disc jockeys that really pushed our big band on radio. Hancock's "Harlem Matinee" show on KGFJ was not so much a jazz show as rhythm and blues. But this program was very popular with the local black community. It also didn't hurt that he had a beautiful black woman named Margie as his co-host and engineer.

From the 1960s on radio changed drastically. To begin with the AM stations started the "chart" system. This boiled down to the fact that if you weren't on a station's chart or playlist on a weekly basis your records would not be played. On the bigger stations pop music completely dominated the airwaves and jazz was pushed out. When FM stations came into the picture, so-called easy listening took over and jazz got shafted again. R & B stations such as KGFJ played the top 40 records on their playlist and didn't vary much from that format. Not until KBCA FM-105, now KKGO, came along as the only commercial jazz station, and the non-commercial public radio, such as KLON at Cal State Long Beach, KXLU at Loyola College, KCRW at Santa Monica Community College, KCSN at Cal State Northridge, KPCC at Pasadena City College, and the Pacifica Foundation's KPFK in Studio City, did Los Angeles get much jazz over the air on radio. Of the non-commercial stations there are a number of excellent programs, but you have to know when they come on since these stations do not play jazz 24 hours. In the commercial sphere, KKGO has a pretty tight playlist these days. After the station changed its call letters in 1982 their format went away from black jazz to a more restricted commercial format. The only other big commercial station that gives a thought to playing jazz is KUTE 102-FM with their "Quiet Storm" format. KTYM, KJLH, and KGFJ AM have all flirted with jazz, but you have to listen long and hard to hear much of anything that could remotely be called jazz.

As far as the nightclub scene goes, it too has changed dramatically over the years. To be honest I stopped going to clubs after I quit playing drums a few years back. I haven't been to a club in so long that I would probably knock on the door to get in. The last club I played was Donte's on Lankershim Boulevard in North Hollywood back in 1972. I played drums again when we made my *Inner Feelings* LP with the Sound Machine in 1975–6, but the very last time I actually played drums was in 1978 for a Sonny Til LP called *Back to the Chapel*. Sonny Til and the Orioles were a famous R & B singing group of the 1950s and 1960s, with hits like *Crying in the Chapel*.

Today there are really only a handful of clubs in the Los Angeles area that consistently feature modern jazz. The Lighthouse out in Hermosa Beach, which has been famous since 1949, is still hanging on. Howard Rumsey, the bassist, has moved from the Lighthouse to Concerts by the Sea in Redondo Beach. Concerts is an attractive club, but because of the current economic climate it seems to favor fusion and lighter fair than I personally enjoy. The Parisian Room on Washington Boulevard in Central LA, which for years was a great place to see everybody from Esther Phillips and Jimmy Witherspoon to Harry "Sweets" Edison and Eddie "Lock-jaw" Davis, has now been closed. Progress in its relentless march has now given us a post office on that corner.

The San Fernando Valley is still a fairly good bet for the club scene. Donte's is still going pretty strong. There's also places like the Money Tree, Le Cafe, and the Baked Potato, though Don Randi favors more fusion and guitar material. Carmelo's used to have some pretty good jazz, but Herb Jeffries recently bought it and changed the name to the Flamingo. He tried to put on only singers and was trying to back every singer with a synthesizer and so now that room has folded.

Marla's Memory Lane here in the inner city will occasionally feature some strong jazz name like Gerald Wilson's big band or Cedar Walton, but the club doesn't really have any sort of coherent booking policy. They had Dizzy there not too long ago but that steep cover charge sent a few people away. Drummer Carl Burnett has opened a small place in central Los Angeles. He's trying to mix it up with shows of jazz artists, poetry readings and occasional one-act plays. He calls it Artworks 4 and it has great potential if Carl can get some publicity going about the space and if the people will support it.

In Hollywood on the Sunset Strip, the Silver Screen room at the Hyatt did a commendable job of featuring jazz. Charles McPherson, Barney Kessel, Tommy Flanagan and Mal Waldron have all played there. Still, the man who booked the room is always getting flack from some new manager who doesn't know anything about the music. The Palace Court on Vine does jazz shows on weekends with locals such as Freddie Hubbard and Horace Tapscott, along with out-of-town players like Art Blakey. Also on Vine is the Vine Street Bar and Grill, which caters to those who enjoy vocalists. Vine Street does a good business and has had Carmen McRae, Anita O'Day, Nancy Wilson and Joe Williams, among many others.

There are a handful of non-profit jazz organizations in town who seem to do good projects in an effort to keep the music alive. Benny Powell's Committee on Jazz has presented concerts in the schools and in parks to children and others who might not get exposed to this music. The Los Angeles Jazz Society has also presented concerts and recently pressured the LA City Council into placing a unique manhole cover in the sidewalk in front of the spot where Shelly Manne's Manne-Hole club used to be in Hollywood on Cahuenga Boulevard. The one organization I am personally aware of is the Jazz Heritage Foundation. They do a number of fund-raising concerts, put out an attractive and informative newsletter and provide scholarships to up-and-coming young musicians who might otherwise not be able to pursue their understanding of this music. Jazz Heritage really does a good job of introducing youngsters to the world of jazz.

This is probably a good beginning as far as trying to reacquaint the public with jazz goes. If you are ever going to get people to support and care about America's only true art form, it seems to me that education is the place to start. This could come about through high-quality publications featuring stories about the lives of jazz musicians and their music – what their backgrounds are, what they've struggled against.

One of the better publications in the United States

featuring interviews, record reviews and news concerning the black jazz experience is *Bebop and Beyond*. *Bebop and Beyond* is a relatively new magazine published bi-monthly here in Los Angeles. It was conceived by four young men that had the idea that the black jazz heritage should be kept alive. *Cadence* magazine is another good bet. This monthly is published in Redwood, New York, and has been around for years with its unique format of interviews, record reviews and LP catalog.

Radio could play an important part in this process. Radio can be all pervasive, since people can listen while they go on about their normal activities. It would be nice to see a few more programs about jazz musicians or jazz concerts such as the public television networks and the cable stations have done on the major network stations. Finally, I'd like to see a more stringent curriculum in the grade schools, high schools and colleges of this country which introduced students to the many faces of this great music and its practitioners.

Today, sad to say, the jazz musician is treated as a third-class citizen in the world of music, a sort of distant step-child of the money-makers in pop, rock and even country. It's difficult to say exactly how or why this pervasive attitude came about. Perhaps we musicians are at least partially at fault, since many of us have succumbed to trying to play what the public thinks jazz is supposed to be. We should have just kept on playing jazz that was true to the individual's vision and let the public catch up with us. It seems to me that only a few artists have done this. Of course economics plays a big part on this process and I don't begrudge anyone that opportunity to earn a good living for their family. But those artists that have remained committed to their own special voice are the ones that we eventually recognize and cherish. On the other hand, this path can be a pretty lonely one, and all too many jazz artists have had to pay some heavy dues for their uncompromising stance about their music. Ironically, even as I sit here mulling all of this over I learn that Horace Tapscott, one of our great classical jazz pianists and a talented composer, has recorded my composition *Jessica* for an album of solo piano works, *The Tapscott Sessions*, vol.6, on Nimbus Records. This makes me quite pleased, and though I don't hear everything that Horace plays I deeply admire him as one of the most committed artists of our time.

In retrospect, I am grateful to be alive, to still be here and to be able to say that I was a part of the many-faceted jazz world.

Finally, I'd like to climb on my soap box and get some things off my chest. Many times I've been called cocky, conceited and controversial, but I have yet to be called a liar about information during the bebop jazz revolution on the West Coast. Since I was here I can document anything I say regarding this issue. The big problem with regard to the history of bebop is that the writers who pass this information along to the public rarely talk to the real bona fide legends of jazz here in Los Angeles. Most times they interview "good musicians" who were here on the edge of the hard-core bebop sets. Consequently, they overlook many of the real pioneers and unsung heroes of bebop jazz.

The film *Bird*, produced and directed by Clint Eastwood, depicting the life of Charlie Parker, is a symbolic example of exploitation of the black artist. The movie is likened to a farce and insults the integrity and intelligence of all black musicians who really knew, lived, worked and recorded with him. Well intentioned it may have been, the fact is that not one of these musicians was consulted concerning *Bird*. They were blatantly ignored and excluded. It would have been advantageous to the film's authenticity to have consulted people who knew the man personally. This would have eliminated the untruths about Bird and some events that did not happen as portrayed in the movie.

It could have been an effort to show the true genius he was. Eastwood surrounded himself with cronies that didn't really know the depth of Charlie Parker. Red Rodney was just another one of a host of white musicians that hung around when and wherever Bird played. It is typical Hollywood whitewash to try and include Whites in that

138 There and Back

movement in jazz. Trying to imply that Rodney's relationship with Charlie Parker was as close as Dizzy Gillespie's is ridiculous. If you didn't really know the facts, it would seem you were watching the "Albino Red" show. Max Roach and Miles Davis played and recorded with Bird more than anyone else. Why weren't they consulted? This was a lackadaisical try about the life of a most complex individual. By dwelling on his narcotic problem, the movie diminished the contribution of his music.

The portrayal of Bird as a drunken, drug addicted, buffoonish and maniacal womanizing saxophone player is degrading. It certainly was not the Charlie Parker I knew. I give Eastwood credit for making the movie but disapprove of the methods. The soundtrack is good, but by removing the original players on *Koko*, *Ornithology*, *Moose the Mooche* and *Lover Man* the feeling was lost. The money and technology used to isolate Bird's solos could have been applied to enhance the sound of the original recordings to fit the sound of that era – hence: the truth. The scene showing Bird throwing his saxophone through the glass window of the control booth while recording *Lover Man* did not happen. I was there. Also, Emry Byrd (Moose the Mooche), the crippled drug dealer, did not ride around in a wheelchair, he walked with crutches and is still alive here in Los Angeles today. I do realize the flair for more dramatics, but why distort the truth? To try and eliminate the other principal innovators and players of that era in jazz, bebop, is pure bigotry and attempted genocide of a culture.

If the movie could have been made without the portrayal of Dizzy Gillespie, it probably would have been. Bebop was totally a black experience, with few Whites participating. It is time to face reality and accept the fact that whatever is filmed or written will not erase the truth of this heritage from history.

The same can be said of many of the jazz societies here. Most of them mean well but fall short of actually honoring the innovators when they honor or give plaques to name jazz artists who really weren't on the scene. Sad to say, these jazz societies know little about what happened in jazz in Los Angeles from the 1940s to the present. Most of the musicians that are members of these societies are really Johnny Come Latelys to LA. I am not putting these people down, but there are really only a few true legends of jazz alive and here today who were on that scene. People like Teddy Edwards, Jimmy Bunn, Dexter Gordon and myself are all innovators. There is a big difference between a good player and an innovator.

Today Charles Mingus, Sonny Criss, Wardell Gray, Hampton Hawes, Leroy "Sweetpea" Robinson and Eric Dolphy are all dead. At the Sunday afternoon jam sessions at Billy Berg's club on Vine Street most of the saxophonists and many of the tenor players like Stan Getz and Zoot Sims would be listening and learning from Theodore Marcus Edwards and Wardell Gray. They would be listening in awe to Teddy, wondering how he could move so fast on his horn, playing the correct chord changes of the tunes. Most people are not aware that Teddy was originally an alto saxophonist and clarinetist – like Sonny Stitt. People like Art Pepper, Joe Maini and even William Green and Buddy Collette were then listening to Sonny Criss and, naturally, Charlie Parker.

Jimmy Bunn was somewhat of a catalyst for quite a few pianists at that time. He was playing the correct chord changes to all the bop tunes quite a while before Hampton Hawes became The Man. Jimmy's attitude and personality caused him problems, as he would just as soon walk off the bandstand if the music wasn't played properly. He is still active around Los Angeles, but he never attained the recognition he deserves.

Clarence Jones and Addison Farmer were the first bass players I saw here in LA that would walk the chord changes of the tunes with all five fingers of the right hand. Most bassists were still pulling and thumping, producing a muffled sound. It is unfortunate that there are no recordings of Clarence Jones. He got caught up early into the use of heroin and died a tragic death from an overdose. Charles Mingus was in a class by himself. Mingus played bass as if it were a guitar, but he was seldom at the hard-core jam session sets. He was mostly practicing or working out lines with the pianist Spaulding Givens or others. Spaulding was another innovator from those times. I don't know what happened to Spaulding, but Mingus left Los Angeles in 1947 with Lionel Hampton. Another fine bassist was Iggy Shevack, who had a good, big sound and was pretty close to the Clarence Jones–Addison Farmer concept, especially when we recorded with Teddy Edwards in 1948 for Rex Records.

A very young Barney Kessel came down to the jam sessions from Hollywood and blew all the guitar players away – all except Big Tiny Webb, that is. Big Tiny looked as if he weighed 300 pounds, but he was bad. Both guitarists learned from each other. Sadly, Tiny died at an early age from health problems caused by obesity. Leo Blevins was another great guitar player. He came here from Chicago and stayed, fitting right into the groove.

On 4 December 1947 Dexter Gordon did his first session for Ross Russell's Dial Records. This set included Jimmy Rowles, piano; Red Callender, bass; and myself, drums. We recorded *Ghost of a Chance*, *Sweet and Lovely*, *Talk of the Town* and *The Duel*, parts 1 & 2, on which Teddy Edwards was added. This gave Ross Russell the chance to get something out on Teddy by himself with a rhythm section – kill two birds with one stone. We did *Blues in Teddy's Flat* that same night and it became a monster seller. Teddy had a 12-bar tenor break with the rhythm section accenting the first beat every two bars. This got all screwed up because Red and Jimmy were trying to listen to what Teddy was playing, instead of counting. It was left up to me to make it come out right. *Blues in Teddy's Flat* made Teddy Edwards well known. I have heard that it was one of the few bebop records that sold a million, besides Charlie Parker's first Dial session.

During this same era, when Howard McGhee had the band at the Finale Club after hours, Shelly Manne, Art Pepper, Bob Cooper, Bud Shank, and Pete and Conte Candoli from Stan Kenton's band were there every morning they were in town, "listening" hard. Don Lamond, Terry Gibbs, Shorty Rogers and the others from the Woody

Herman Herd were there too. But truthfully, all the innovations and contributions to the field of jazz were made by black musicians who have paid some heavy dues. Most all of the rest were just carbon copies of the real thing. This has been the case from the beginning. There have always been good, schooled white musicians that sound good, but that's not the same as making a contribution.

Most all drummers were trying to emulate Max Roach, Art Blakey and myself. All along we had some very talented youngsters blossoming on the scene, such as Lawrence Marable, Leroy McCray, Johnny Lawson, Nat Meeks, and Art and Addison Farmer. By the time I organized my big band in 1948, the new crop of gifted musicians was emerging. Walter Benton, Vi Redd, Clora Bryant, Lavonne Tyus and Frank Morgan were coming to the forefront in the youngster category. Clifford Solomon, Hadley Caliman, Boogie Daniels, Sweetpea Robinson and Eric Dolphy were all members of the Roy Porter Big Band, as were a very young Chet Baker and Herb Geller for a short period.

The Roy Porter Big Band added an important dimension to the history of this music – namely camaraderie and unity, with a great deal of love and respect. This undertaking was a labor of love and was really a horse of another color, since musicians of all races flocked to the rehearsals of this new big band in town. As the band started to show promise, musicians from Hollywood could not be kept away from the rehearsals. Jive-ass A & R men from jive-ass record companies, phoney managers and promoters, all sorts of vocalists – both male and female – and even musicians that heretofore had hardly wanted to speak to me, were all on hand. It was quite an experience for us youngsters.

I'd also like to add my first-hand recollections to what has been written about the Central Avenue music scene in Los Angeles. What made Central Avenue so different was the variety of music which the clubs provided. At the Down Beat Club, Howard McGhee played for four to six weeks. Then Joe Liggins and the Honeydrippers came in for another four to six weeks. Across the street, the Last Word had Slim

Gaillard appearing, while the Club Alabam had Johnny Otis's big Basie-sounding band, along with T-Bone Walker and a floor show. This was all going on at the same time and was very exciting.

Meanwhile the migratory process was beginning. Some musicians from Los Angeles trekked to New York and many of the eastern musicians "caught the covered wagons" out west to Los Angeles. Most made LA their home because of the lifestyle, the weather and the possibilities of recording and studio work.

Jazz is still evolving and is today striving for more recognition from the general public. But, as Gil Scott-Heron said, "The revolution will not be televised." I know for damn sure the music revolution was not.

9

Colleagues

CLORA BRYANT

Reminiscing with Roy I realized that he had played in my home town of Denison, Texas, when he was in the Wiley Collegians. The Collegians also used to play my old school, Prairie View, at homecoming football games. Those were happy, care-free times, even though there was a war going on.

But the first time that I personally met Roy was in 1946 at the Down Beat Club on Central Avenue. At that time I was heavily into the Central Avenue scene and there were sessions up and down the street. Central Avenue was then just what the name implies – a central area, the core or center for all black entertainers. Roy was the drummer with the Down Beat house band. It was led by Howard McGhee on trumpet, with Teddy Edwards on sax, J. D. King on sax, Dingbod Kesterson on bass and Vernon Biddle on piano. Since I only lived a few blocks away I'd walk to all the clubs. I was living with Doris Jarrett, a bass player, who'd asked her mom to let me share her home. At that time you didn't have to worry about being attacked and it was safe to walk the streets at night alone.

My first impression of Roy was, "Gee, he's such a small, thin young man to play the drums with such definition and authority." I also said, "He's such a handsome, small young man." Looks came second at that time because I was more interested in all the musical sounds that I heard around me rather than eyeballing the young men who were making the sounds. Don't get me wrong: reckless eyeballing had its place in my life. But music was then and has always been the first thing to get my attention, after my family, of course.

I remember the way Roy sat at the drums. He'd sit there with a naughty twinkle in his eyes, a little slouch in his back and shoulders, his head tilted slightly to the right, and all the while those devilish eyes would be searching, darting, scanning the room for the pretty young things who made the clubs a beehive of female activity. Then, when he made eye-to-eye contact, he'd zero in and the look would become dark and piercing. In fact, he could undress you and make love to you in one single glance. But Roy never gave me those looks. I wonder why, Roy?

But I remember how good that group sounded. I felt that music to my toes. I'd sit at a table with one glass of Coca-Cola all night. I made it a point to know all of the waitresses in all of the clubs on a first-name basis, and they in turn would let me sit there without hustling me. Sometimes Pops, the owner, would be hound-dogging them and they'd bring me another Coke and pay for it themselves. They knew I didn't have the money. Or one of the musicians would buy me a soda, since by that time they all knew me. Those were some beautiful, heady, musically fulfilling nights, Sunday afternoons, and early-morning sessions.

I saw Roy at different places, but by 1947 I was working with an all-girl group, the Four Queens, with Elyse Blye, piano, Doris Jarrett, bass, and Minnie Hightower, sax. On one gig I had to play drums and trumpet at the same time, and, yes, I was influenced by Roy's drumming. I'd played my Dial records of Charlie Parker with Roy Porter. (I too had trouble counting Bird's famous four-bar break on *Night in Tunisia*.) Well, when we got this job at the Onyx Club in Pasadena on Fair Oaks, where we needed a drummer, I volunteered to do the job. I went to Lockie's music store downtown and rented some drums. On bass we had a young man named George Morrow, the same George Morrow who later became famous when he was with the Clifford Brown–Max Roach group.

In 1947 I started dating my future husband, Joe Stone, who

became the bass player in Roy's big bebop band in 1948. I still left some time for reckless eyeballing, but always after my music.

When Joe went with Sonny Criss's group in 1950, with Roy and Hampton Hawes, to the Wolf Club in Oakland, I came up and stayed for a week or two at Joe's cousin's house. By then we were married and had a son, Charles Batiste. Joe was really gung-ho about the group. He'd go to work at night and then play at the early-morning sessions. By the time he got home I'd be up with the baby. I'd fix him something to eat and he'd tell me all the exciting things that the band was doing. He knew how I loved every little detail. When they went to Bop City I had to leave. The girl group I was with had two jobs waiting in Phoenix and Las Vegas.

By the time Joe and I were back again in LA he had more exciting things to tell me about the group. How they would "swing everybody into bad health" and how Roy was really "putting the pots on." Everyone came by Bop City.

I lost track of Roy while he was in Chino. When he came out in 1956 we were able to resume our friendship because they released him in LA.

A few years after our daughter, April Michon, was born Joe and I separated. Roy and I started to work together at the Rag Doll in North Hollywood with Sigmund Galloway on sax, Henry McDade on piano and Eddie Davis on bass. The group was together and the Rag Doll was a lot of fun. It was great playing with Roy, my favorite drummer on the gig. Sometimes he'd give me rides home, but he didn't give me those eyes; he had so many girlfriends then.

I was disappointed when Roy left the group to go with Louis Jordan. The night Louis came to recruit Roy he offered me a job too, but I had to decline. When Roy got to Vegas with Louis he met and married Tina, the mother of his only son, Daryl. And now Daryl has made him a grand-father. Roy's as happy as a lark with his grand-daughter, Daryl Nieanna.

Roy and I keep in touch. When my friends gave a benefit for me in 1983 when I lost my home, Roy was there with financial and moral support. That's what friendship is about. I have lots of acquaintances, but Roy is one of my friends.

GEORGE "RED" CALLENDER

Roy and I were on a number of record dates during the 1940s. Some of these were *Blues in Teddy's Flat*, with Teddy Edwards; *The Duel*, with Dexter Gordon and Teddy Edwards; and the famous jam session in 1947 at the Elks Auditorium with Dexter, Wardell Gray, Howard McGhee, Trummy Young, Hampton Hawes, Barney Kessel and Sonny Criss. *Jeronimo* was released from this session. Unfortunately, I don't seem to have any tapes of the different times that Roy and I worked together, because since then I've moved about quite a lot. However, I do remember that we were also playing together on the Joe Liggins *Honeydripper* album, recorded in the early 1960s.

Roy was always a swinging drummer, way ahead of the times we were playing in. Some drummers were into a heavy bass drum still, but Roy was into the new styles developing at that time.

CHARLOTTE COLLINS (BANKS)

In the 1940s, when I was in San Diego, I had the pleasure of seeing Roy Porter again for a few treasured hours. He was featured with his band at a local ballroom. I waited in a block-long line to get a ticket. When I finally entered the dance hall, I saw Roy on the bandstand on his throne – amid a royal set of drums.

Roy and I grew up in Colorado Springs, a resort town that hibernated in the winter. Roy lived on the south side of town with his sister Evelyn and his mother. It was his mother, Charlotte Porter, who instilled education, honesty, dignity, courage and ambition in Roy which he brought with him into the music world.

Back there, in order to keep in touch with the jazz world, we had to go to Denver – to Five Points or the Rainbow

Ballroom, which featured all the famous bands: Duke Ellington, Gene Krupa, Cab Calloway. It was during that time that Roy must have caught the stimulus of the music that took control of his life.

I visited his mother the day after Roy left for Wiley College in Marshall, Texas. Despite his scholastic abilities, Roy didn't get a scholarship. In those days they were hard to come by if you were black. He wasn't in the right clique either to get one from the church. But, despite it all, sheer guts and determination sent Roy to college. He packed his suitcase, piled his drums on the train and took off.

"He's got nerve," his mother stated emphatically, "nerve, ability and lots of determination."

I wondered aloud what would happen if he didn't make it.

Charlotte Porter laughed, "Oh, he'll make it alright. He has to. He doesn't have money to come back on." Her concern was deep, however. She loved her son dearly, and knew he was special.

Mrs Porter, a devout Christian, was kind and very generous. But most of all it was her infectious laugh, her understanding and encouragement which she offered so freely. She was a great lady and some of her attributes are still strong in Roy. Once she told me, in that amusing way that she had, "I bought Roy a clarinet, and just listen to him back there in his room beating on those tin cans."

I wished she could have heard Roy that night in San Diego; that moment should have been reserved for her. Roy was elegant – a gentleman – a sensation. Dignity and pride was still strong. He was in his glory, charming and alive. When he soloed the crowd went wild. Electricity filled the room. Roy gave a brilliant rendition – a startling reality that everyone had waited for. And when it was over he stood to a standing ovation.

CLYDE DUNN

Joe Howard, who was with me in Roy's big band, and I met in September 1946, the first day of school at Jefferson High in

LA. Joe was originally from Marshall, Texas. I had gone to grammar school and junior high school at Grambling College in Louisiana. Joe was the cause of me playing baritone sax. When school opened my horn was still in the shop being overhauled, since my father had taken my silver tenor sax to be gold lacquered when we came to California. At school someone had given the swing band a new bari sax and no one wanted to play it. Everyone who tried didn't notice that the reed was off-center on the mouthpiece. Joe showed me how to straighten the reed and play the baritone sax. I never got to play tenor again until 1959.

Our teacher, Samuel Brown, had written an arrangement on the song *It Might as Well be Spring* for Paul Sparks to sing. Paul later became the vocalist with Roy's band and can be heard on some of the records.

Joe Howard arranged many of the songs that made the Roy Porter band what is now a 35-year-old institution. Roy's band members had a great love for each other, from the valet Cisco to Sweetpea, Art Farmer, Eric Dolphy, Eddie Preston, Jimmy Knepper, Robert Ross and through Roy. We were the first big-band beboppers.

TEDDY EDWARDS

Roy and I have remained good friends over the years. We both worked together with Howard McGhee and we recorded different things together as well as playing on many jam sessions.

Roy's putting together a big band of largely unproven players was a bold undertaking. Fortunately, he had plenty of good talent to work with. Most importantly, he had a couple of fine young arrangers in Joe Howard and Robert Ross.

In 1948 I had written a composition entitled *Sunset Eyes* for an early television pilot. Later I orchestrated it for the band. To this day I still use that same arrangement when I play that tune. Robert Ross made a fine arrangement of another song of mine called *Roy's Boy*, which we'd recorded in 1947.

Roy's big band had great spirit and every time they got together it was like a big party. I enjoyed it very much then and am glad that there is still some recorded and photographic evidence of it around today.

ART FARMER

When I first met Roy he was playing with what I thought was the best jazz group on the West Coast. It was a sextet led by Howard McGhee, and Roy was one of the top drummers on the coast that could play in the new style and still swing. Later, after Dizzy Gillespie came out with his group, with Charlie Parker, Roy made some recordings and some gigs with Parker.

The scene in Los Angeles at that time was very alive, with clubs on Central Avenue and after-hours places featuring small jazz groups. At these establishments there were a lot of jam sessions, and young musicians could get to hear and play with their idols – it was a chance to learn by doing. However, there was something missing and that was a rehearsal band. At Jefferson High School there was a dance band, but one had to be a student there to play in that band. Gerald Wilson, Floyd Ray and other leaders organized bands from time to time when there was work, but there was no steady organized big band for the younger musicians such as myself to play in and really learn how to play with modern big bands. Roy got the idea to organize a big band, I think, after Dizzy came out west with his big band. Anyway, I was there from the start and it was a great opportunity for me.

The writers Joe Howard and Robert Ross were writing very modern arrangements that were a challenge to play, and by playing them I was able to prepare myself for future work with bands such as Benny Carter, Gerald Wilson, Lionel Hampton, etc. There were other exceptional players in the band, among them Eric Dolphy, and others that were also very good but never gained the prominence that Eric did. Leroy "Sweetpea" Robinson was an alto sax player who was quite good. Joe Howard the arranger was also a gifted tenor player, while the other tenor man was Hadley Caliman. Hadley could play very well too. These were the main soloists in the band, along with myself and, of course, Roy.

We played a few dates around the LA area for very small money, but the experience was worth much more than any money that was being paid anywhere. This was the time when the big-band era was coming to an end, excluding the very famous, and so opportunities to gain experience were scarce.

Someone put some dates together for the Porter band in the South-west and we left by autos to make them. We played our first date in Phoenix, Arizona. Our next date was to have been El Paso, Texas, but there was an accident in the auto Roy and I were in. We would up in the hospital and the tour was canceled. I don't remember playing with the band after that.

Before the accident we did some recording for Savoy Records, which I believe are the first recordings I did; at least it was the first time that I got to play a solo on a recording date. This was before tape came into use, so there was no splicing. If the band played a song all the way to the end and then someone made a mistake, we just had to start all the way back at the beginning. We didn't imagine any other way, so no one complained, but all tried their best to get through their part without making mistakes.

One of the jobs I remember well was a dance at the place we used for our rehearsals. It was called the Chicken Shack. Someone had the idea for us to play a New Year's Eve dance there. We played it, but whoever was holding the cigar box with the paid admissions took almost all of the money and disappeared. We wound up with next to nothing and I personally received 20 cents. But we were all young and such things didn't linger too long in our consciousness. We were all thinking more about the future than about the present.

DONNA JEAN GENTRY

I first heard of Roy Porter when he was working the Down

Beat Club on Central Avenue with Howard McGhee's band, but I didn't actually meet him until some time later.

I came to Los Angeles from Memphis, Tennessee, in 1946. I was born in Memphis, went to school there, and started to dance there. I knew Sonny Criss in Memphis from when we were kids of nine years old. He went to Florida Street School and I went to Korchet Intermediate School. Our mothers were good friends, though we didn't live in the same neighborhoods. There were many musicians and entertainers in Memphis, and a lot of them would rehearse at our house. That was a big influence on me at that age, and that made me want to become a dancer. Jimmie Lunceford's big band played dances and clubs there and his wife was one of my school teachers.

Los Angeles in 1946 was very exciting to me, so pretty and *big*; the weather was so nice, and there was always so much going on. So I stayed. At first I was working in Roy Milton's grocery store as a cashier. The store was located at First Street and I was living at the Civic Hotel on the corner of First and San Pedro. Estelle Edson, Teddy Edwards, Gene Montgomery and Charlie Parker also lived there. Down the street was Shep's Playhouse, where Leonard Reed was producing shows.

One day some dancing girls came into the store to buy some sodas. I met Frances Neely and told her that I was a dancer. She told Norma Miller about me, and I was hired as one of the dancers at the Club Alabam. Johnny Otis had the big band there, and the show was always good. I eventually married Lee Wesley Jones, his piano player.

Dinah Washington, Joyce Bryant, Claude Trenier, Redd Foxx & Slappy White, T-Bone Walker, Billy Eckstine, Dizzy Gillespie and many more all came through the Alabam. The Norma Miller Dancers were the chorus line at the shows. The chorus line at that time consisted of a male singer nicknamed Peter Rabbit, along with Alice Lyons, Flick Montgomery, myself, Louise Collette, Pudgy, Norma Miller, and another male dancer, André.

At that time Lee Wesley and I lived in the backhouse on 47th Street off Broadway, and Buddy Collette and Louise lived in the front. We all used to joke about Buddy, because he would come over to our house and practice his instrument *all the time*, but never did get a job, while my husband Lee Wesley was always working. Now Buddy Collette is one of the highest-paid saxophone players in the country.

I first met Roy when he came by another place we had on 55th Street near Avalon to talk to Lee Wesley about some music. But it wasn't until much later in the 1960s that I got to know Roy. He'd just written *Lonesome Mood* and it was out locally by a group called the Vocals. Later, when the Friends of Distinction recorded it in 1969, it was a hit. I owned a record store on Adams Boulevard and Roy brought *Lonesome Mood* by to see what I thought of it. I'd heard it before, but really enjoyed the Friends' job on it and told him that I thought it was one of the most beautiful songs I'd heard. I still love that song.

From that point on we became good friends, and remain so today. We'd talk and we found that many of the people Roy knew I also knew. We reminisced about Stuff Smith, the first jazz violinist, whom I'd worked with in St Louis and Roy had worked with on Hollywood Boulevard; T-Bone Walker; Sammy Yates, a very good trumpet player from Chicago; Dinah Washington, whom we both knew; and Clarence Jones, a great local bassist, and my premonition of his death and its circumstances.

Later, when Roy made the *Jessica* album with his Sound Machine, he was surprised to know that I knew Louis Polieman Brown. Brown was a Nigerian conga drummer and was on one cut on the LP called *Drums for Daryl*. I'd worked with Louis and Lee Shamburger on many jobs. But Louis did a lot of movies. Sometimes when we worked it would just be the two of us. He'd play drums and I'd dance. Louis died before he got to hear Roy's album and his death was a shock to both of us.

Today the entertainment field is much different. Then, big bands on stage with a floor show featuring chorus girls and comedians was the big thing. Most of the big theaters and nightclubs had a show to present and it was all great fun. I know this book is mostly about musicians, but without the dancing show-girls there would have been no show.

JIMMY KNEPPER
trombone, arranger

I knew Roy Porter from the Howard McGhee band, which also had Teddy Edwards and Bird in it, after Bird got out of Camarillo. In 1948 Roy put a big band together for a record date with Savoy Records. We rehearsed daily for weeks. Most of what I remember was of California port wine. Before each rehearsal there was an amassing of money: ten cents, seven cents, a quarter, or whatever to get enough for the wine. Wiggie, William Wiginton, one of our trombonists, had a tune that I arranged entitled *Stalled Horse* and another one called *Phantom Moon*, which was recorded for the Savoy session. Kenny Bright, a trumpet player, did a tune and arrangement called *Moods at Dusk*, which was recorded in 1950 on another record date by Roy.

A few years later I was at LA City College with Eric Dolphy, who was also a member of Roy's band. We'd play sections of Stravinsky's *L'Histoire du soldat*, and at that point Eric was into clarinet. Joe Maini was also in the Roy Porter band. After I sold my wire recorder to Reuben McFall, another trumpet player in the band, Joe and I were in Denver with the Glenn Henry Band. From there we hitched to New York (another story). Luckily, Reuben sent installment payments for the wire recorder to New York, which came in the nick of time for our eating purposes. Joe and I later played in "the band that never was," a huge band Gene Roland put together for Charlie Parker to lead. From this association, Bird hired me to play with him in Philadelphia at the Showboat Lounge. That was a highlight in my life. Bird also used to come to our infamous basement apartment at 136th and Broadway.

During one of those rehearsals with the Roy Porter big band earlier in LA, Wayne Harris, our bassist, got his girlfriend to give us a lift after the rehearsal. I didn't really meet her till two years later in New York, and a few years after we married.

There were more, but I can only remember one job at the Elks Hall in LA, aside from the three record dates. Now after 30 years they've released some of that material, but it's too bad that the band never got backing or a foothold as it was full of love, talent and wine.

LAWRENCE MARABLE

I remember the first time I saw Roy at the Down Beat. He was at a jam session there with Hampton Hawes, Benny Bailey, Dexter Gordon and Addison Farmer. They were playing tunes like *Idaho*, *Cherokee*, *How High the Moon* and other jam standards. They'd play them so fast and they'd stay that way all night long. I couldn't believe it. I was 16 then, and Bill, the guy at the door, would always put me out because I was under age. I'd go out the front door and sneak right through the back again. I'd heard the songs that they were playing on radio, but to see guys actually playing them was amazing. Then I'd say, "I'm going to do that one day." Those times at the Down Beat were great and I'll never forget when Roy took time with me to show me things. Actually, Roy first showed me how to hold a drumstick.

At that time it seemed like the musicians were more friendly and that there was more camaraderie between them all. They were also more helpful to the youngsters who were just coming along. The drummers who really took some time with me, besides Roy, were Chuck Thompson and Tim Kennedy. Thompson was from LA, while Kennedy was a drummer from Detroit who'd moved here.

At the Down Beat I'd sit for hours watching and learning, until they put me out. Roy had a cymbal with rivets in it that got such a different sound that all he had to do was play that cymbal and it would just knock me out.

Meanwhile I'm still listening to the radio, hearing Artie Shaw, Benny Goodman and Tommy Dorsey. I remember a disc jockey named Hunter Hancock who was broadcasting from some little fish-frying station with his program "Harlem Matinee." (A fish-frying station was one which did not have a strong signal, and typically possessed a static-filled one.) That was the first time I heard a record by Teddy Edwards with Benny Bailey, Duke Brooks, Addison Farmer and Roy Porter. The stuff they were playing was was ahead of its time.

A bit later, when I got a chance to play with some of these guys, it was a blast. Gene Montgomery, a tenor saxophone player, ran the sessions at the Down Beat and let me play. So I went on and "burned" as much as I could at that time. I kept practicing and the guys liked me and I started playing with them. But I quickly found out that seeing these cats perform and physically playing myself were two different things. I'd thought it would be easy, but I quickly found out I didn't have the stamina and it took lots of hard work for me to get to that point where these pros were.

RUDY PITTS

I had never met Roy Porter until I came to the West Coast in 1947 with King Kolax, who also had John Coltrane in the band. Bird was out here then, and Roy Porter had made some sides with Bird for Dial Records. In King Kolax's big band we only listened to Bird, Diz and Miles, etc., so I really dug Roy on those sides with Bird. When Roy first saw me he knew me and I knew him, or something like that.

A bit later Roy put together his big band. I'd been back east and was heading west and stopped off in Phoenix, Arizona. There I got the chance to hear Roy's band, which had a real big sound. At that time R & B was the big thing – Big Jay McNeely, Roy Milton, and T-Bone Walker, etc. But Roy's big band had that jazz sound and it really swung. When they left Phoenix the band had a car accident and some of the guys were hurt and hospitalized. Thank God no one was killed.

I went to his rehearsals and I used to see Roy sitting in the back of the band, where he had to direct, call tunes and signal this or that section. Drummers had always sat back there in the rhythm. I told him that with all of the directing he was doing he should bring his drums down front and let me play the drums when he was directing and working with his trumpet or sax players. I worked in the band as a drummer and that music we played was good jazz.

TINA CECELIA COLLINS PORTER

I've known Roy Porter as man, father, musician, drummer, writer, composer, arranger and a truly great human being. I am happy to have been a part of his past, to be a part of his present, and a part of his future. All because of a common bond that we have – our son Daryl Roy Porter and our grand-daughter, Daryl Nieanna Porter.

Roy and I met and married in Las Vegas in 1957 and were separated and divorced in 1968. The ten years we were together were not the best. And yet they were not the worst. There were good and bad times. But for the most part, I've always had great admiration and respect for Roy.

Back in the 1940s I used to see Roy quite often, going to and fro on Central Avenue. At that time I was not into music so much, but I did know who he was.

One night at a jam session at Jack's Basket Room on Central Avenue I met Roy and Teddy Edwards through a friend. At that time little did I know what was in the future regarding Roy and me. I never had a chance to hear Roy's big band in person, but I was continually hearing all the records he'd made with other people. I was aware of his career, but he was just another musician to me.

I lost track of Roy for quite a few years, until I saw him in Las Vegas at the Cotton Club in the casino, where I was writing keno. I never will forget the way he approached me, because he had forgotten he'd met me before in LA. His come-on was, "Hey, little girl. What's your name with your big pretty legs?"

I said to myself, "Who does this dude think he's talking this trash to?"

Anyway, we got friendly and started playing keno together. We won some money and eventually became good friends. He asked me to come to the Sands to see him in the show with Louis Jordan. I said OK, and he gave me his phone number at the motel. When he walked away, I threw the number in the trash can. The next night he asked me why I didn't show. I told him that I didn't go to shows by myself. He was quite perturbed, but did ask me to visit him at his motel, so I finally did after some more time went by. I noticed then that he was drinking heavily and I invited him to my home for a talk. I told him that I knew about his drug addiction and incarceration for drugs. I said that if he could beat a drug habit, he could beat anything. He told me that I was right and that he'd try. We fell in love and he asked me to marry him, but the first time he proposed I said no. The second time I agreed and we were married by a justice of the peace in Las Vegas in January 1957.

When we got to the justice of the peace, there were many people sitting around waiting to get married. But Roy came in so boisterous and asked the man, "How much do you charge for me to marry the woman I love?" When he said that all the people who were waiting nervously started having a ball with each other. That remark loosened everyone up.

Roy was leaving the next day, so we made our plans for me to come to Los Angeles and begin our married life together. I noticed that he kept drinking heavily and that he kept saying that he was trying to quit, but it seemed to me that he wasn't trying hard enough. I knew that he was on Miltown, an anti-depressant, and that he was not supposed to drink with this medication. But what I didn't realize was that he was so sick with his migraine headaches. It saddens me that all through our marriage his drinking was a problem. We had no money problems, but the alcohol made him abusive and I couldn't take that.

Since Roy and I have been divorced we have remained friends, and have collaborated on songs together. We also have our own publishing company for our music. And whenever it is necessary, we will do anything for one another.

I've had my doubts about Roy coming out of all that he has

gone through. He's paid his dues to the hilt. But I am just so happy and proud that he has proven me wrong. He's still a nut. And he still tries to boss me around as if he were my father. But it's a good feeling to know that someone always cares for you. I pray that he will have continuous success in his endeavors and God speed ahead.

EDDIE PRESTON

I met Roy at Wiley College in Marshall, Texas, where we were room-mates. McKinley Dorham, Wild Bill Davis and Russell Jacquet were also at Wiley then. Bill Davis was doing the writing for the Wiley Collegians Orchestra. Kinney, Roy and I were freshmen and I didn't make the band the first year because the band was set before I arrived. So I became the band boy. Roy was the mainstay in the band and we got along well. The band traveled all over Texas for weekend dances and "Battles of the Bands." I didn't return to Wiley College the second year, so I didn't see Roy again for about three years, when I arrived in Los Angeles with the Ernie Fields Orchestra, which featured Teddy Edwards on alto saxophone. I'd been traveling with different bands since Wiley, mainly with Hot Lips Page's orchestra, which took me to New York City. I'd also been on the road with the Conny Connell Band, which included Thad Jones, who was a lot of help to me in my learning stage.

I decided to stay in Los Angeles at the Club Alabam, working with the Johnny Otis Big Band. I called Roy, of course, and we stayed in contact with each other. In between rehearsals with Roy's band and working with Johnny Otis, I enrolled at UCLA for a semester. Then I started traveling again.

After touring with Johnny Otis and the Ink Spots, and going to Hawaii with Cee Pee Johnson, Red Callender, Trummy Young, Dexter Gordon and others, I returned to Los Angeles and spent most of my time with the Roy Porter Orchestra. His band featured musicians like Art Farmer, Jimmy Knepper, Eric Dolphy, Addison Farmer and my cousin Paul Sparks on vocals. Incidentally, Art Farmer was with me on part of the Johnny Otis tour. I didn't see Eric Dolphy or Jimmy Knepper any more for years until I came east and we worked together with Charles Mingus.

The scene in LA in the middle and late 1940s was very exciting and I was glad to be part of the Roy Porter Big Band and that whole experience. It was an excellent band with good personnel and good arrangements as well as some fine soloists. I think that the music we played in the 1940s is still the music of today and the future. It was modern then and still sounds good today.

There was plenty of work around Los Angeles then – regular gigs, after-hours gigs, jam sessions, etc. Our band worked mostly on the east side at places like the Last Word, the Down Beat, the Open Door, the Club Alabam and Jack's Basket Room, all of which were on Central Avenue. We had sessions at all these clubs, and on Sundays Billy Berg's was the place to be. These jam sessions featured Charlie Parker, Dexter Gordon, Wardell Gray, Miles Davis, Von Streeter, Paul Quinichette, Sonny Criss, Hampton Hawes, Buddy Collette, Al Killian, Freddie Simon and so many others. This was before rock and disco. There was nothing but good music around. I consider myself fortunate to have been a part of this scene and thank the Lord for being at the right place at the right time. This scene and the knowledge that I received with the Roy Porter band prepared me for the bands of Count Basie, Duke Ellington, Lionel Hampton, and all the others that I worked for.

MAURICE SIMON

I first heard of Roy Porter in Houston, Texas. He was with the Wiley Collegians and they played the El Dorado Ballroom in Third Ward. Later Roy was a member of Milton Larkin's orchestra from Houston. Next, we met out in Los Angeles in the mid-1940s when Roy was with the Howard McGhee–Charlie Parker band, which was playing down at the Club Finale.

At that time I was with the Gerald Wilson Orchestra, playing baritone and tenor saxophones. When we'd finish a gig we'd all jam the nights away at places like Jack's Basket Room on Central. On stage at Jack's there'd be Gene Montgomery, Teddy Edwards, Sonny Criss, Shifty Henry, Roy, Wardell Gray, Dexter Gordon, Hampton Hawes and others.

Roy's big band from this same time period was popular, but short-lived. He'd chosen some of the best up-and-coming musicians, like Eric Dolphy (with whom I'd attended Dorsey High School in 1944–5) and Clyde Dunn (who was in my class at Jefferson High in 1946). Roy also had Art Farmer and his twin brother Addison in that band.

Later Roy moved up to San Francisco, where he was in the company of Dizzy, Bird and Miles – the cats who were doing it. I, on the other hand, stayed with a lot of big bands, working with Illinois Jacquet, Billy Williams, Cootie Williams, Cab Calloway and Earl Gray. My brother Freddie was another section man, and before his death he was a featured member in Lionel Hampton's big band on tenor saxophone.

In 1969 Roy formed a group called Sound Machine which played the Yamashiro Skyroom in the Hollywood Hills. We stayed there for a year and a half and had a ball.

HENRY SMITH

It was one of those days when everything was going right for me. On 8 March 1949 I met Roy Porter for the first time. It all began as usual over lunch at the Dunbar Grill on Central Avenue. This was a gathering place where musicians and entertainers met to talk about new gigs.

As I was walking down the avenue towards the Down Beat Club, a friend stopped me and asked if I was going in there. "Go on. Don't miss a treat. There's a rehearsal going on at the old Chinese Theater at 29th and Central Avenue," he said. Being an A & R person for a record company named Knockout Records, I couldn't resist something like this, and, typical of the others of our breed, my blood began to pound away. So, hence I went.

After reaching the club, I heard a sound – what a sound! My A & R instincts told me that my friend was right. The sound was so incredible that I told myself that I had to go in there and see who was making musical history. When I reached the door of the club, I was told that rehearsal was closed to the public, but, like the publicity hounds before me, I was determined that I wasn't going to let anything stop me. I gave this person at the door my card and asked to see the head honcho of the group. Shortly thereafter I was invited in by the leader, the drummer. That was Roy. One of the first things I noticed was how large the band was: 17 musicians. So, it was from that first meeting and a shared musical appreciation that Roy and I became very good friends.

After a few more visits to hear the band, I asked Roy if he would like to record for my company, Knockout Records. He agreed, and they recorded *Moods at Dusk, Sampson's Creep, Hunter's Hunters* and *Blues à la Carte*.

When Roy returned to LA in 1957 I'd formed Debonair Records with my partner Carl Leftwich and decided to record Roy again. The fervor for big bands was dying down, and they were becoming fewer and fewer. Now it was small combos. I collaborated with Roy on forming a small group under his leadership. It was a quintet and he was playing organ. Roy went along with the project since he had complete control over the songs played. The organ was something new for Roy. He'd never played it before, but I suspected that, as talented as he was, it wasn't going to be all that hard for him.

Once we got the quintet going, we selected the songs to record, which were all written and arranged by Roy. We worked on the sound, but Roy decided that he wanted to spend some more time on it. He worked on it for a few days over at Universal Studios in Hollywood until he finally got the right sound. When he felt comfortable with it we did the recording session. The group recorded *Love You, Got a Funny*

Feelin', *Wow* and *Minor Mood*. The last song was later changed to *Lonesome Mood* and became a hit.

CLIFFORD SOLOMON

I was born in 1931 on the east side of LA, but my family moved to Watts, which was then considered a separate part of the city. I started playing clarinet in 1943 but in 1944 I switched to saxophone because all of the guys were playing it. What really made me change my mind was an appearance by Nat Cole at an assembly in Jordan Junior High or High. This was before Nat became a superstar. This performance was nice, but one of the groups that got all of us really excited about the new word "bebop" was Howard McGhee's band with Teddy Edwards, J. D. King, Vernon Biddle and Roy Porter. Some of my other classmates at Jordan were Tony Ortega, Paul Madison, Walter Benton, Cecil McNeely and William "Boogie" Daniels.

There was a very good saxophone player named Pete Kinard who opened up a record store in the neighborhood then. We'd all hang out there and that's the place where I first heard Charlie Parker. The records were *Congo Blues*, *Get Happy*, *Hallelujah* and *Salt Peanuts*, with Dizzy Gillespie.

But Teddy Edwards was the one who turned all the dudes around on saxophone. Plus, he was always such a beautiful person. You could call Teddy at four in the morning and he would help you on your horn with the correct changes to *Cherokee*. Some other people didn't want to be bothered, but Teddy would always take the time to show saxophone players the right way. Teddy is surely one of the most underrated players today. Outside of Dexter and Wardell he was my biggest influence. Sonny Criss was living off 103rd and Mary Avenue in 1945–6. Another big influence on my playing was Cecil McNeely, later called Big Jay McNeely. He was a hell of a bebop player, until he found a way to make some money by being the "Deacon Hopper." He could really play his ass off. Big Jay and Sonny both switched schools from Jordan to Jefferson High because they wanted to study under Sam Brown, the legendary musical instructor.

I attended Los Angeles High. Hampton Hawes went to Polytechnic, as did Sonny Criss for a bit. Eric Dolphy was at Dorsey. You had to go to school in your district, but we all had a common bond in music. Samuel Brown was the catalyst for so many young musicians like Dexter Gordon, the Farmer brothers and many more.

About the time I started playing music there was the Down Beat Club on 42nd and Central and the Last Word across the street. Nardoni Bates had a record store on 41st and Central with a piano in his back room. So since we were always trying out new musical things, places like Nardoni's where we could play became our hangouts. We would jam all day. Cats like Art Farmer, Willie Smith (who was also known as Billy when he recorded later with Monk) and Nat Meeks would bring in bebop lines and play for hours.

When Nardoni Bates's record shop folded we moved over to Sweetpea Robinson's house. His mother had a big house near 40th and Central. In the back was a garage which Leroy had converted into a practice room, complete with piano. It seemed like everybody came by there. We'd also go into all the little beer joints that had pianos and ask the owner to let us play jam sessions. We'd explain that he didn't have to pay us and could just charge 50 cents on the door and we'd take that. All of our friends usually came by and so the owner would sell some beer and be happy. We took the door, and even if there was only two or three dollars we were happy because we just wanted to play.

The first time I saw Roy was, as I mentioned, with Howard McGhee at Jordan Junior High School. Later I caught him at the Down Beat nightclub. We didn't play together until I joined Roy's big band in 1948. But Roy first heard me playing at the Down Beat during their jam sessions on either a Sunday afternoon or a Monday night. That band had Lawrence Marable, Leroy McCray, and Jimmy "Snake" O'Brien on piano, along with myself on sax. Gene Montgomery ran those jam sessions and he'd let all of the young cats who could play get up on stage.

I enjoyed playing in Roy's big band and have to mention one little historical note. In the Eric Dolphy biography by

Vladimir Simosko and Barry Tepperman they write that I said that the Roy Porter big band was "riddled" with junkies. This is just a damn lie. No one even talked to me about this. During that time all we were doing was drinking white port wine and lemon juice, because Cisco, our valet, liked that vino. It was part of Cisco's job to keep us supplied with wine, and once in a while we'd have some bennies and maybe a little weed. But Cisco did this job better than anything else he was supposed to be doing. Eric Dolphy himself did not do anything. And, for the record, hard-stuff use did not even start around here until 1950 or 1951.

I think Roy got the idea for his big band after he'd seen some of the young cats at the jam sessions at the Crystal Tearoom on 48th and Avalon. Those that could *play* ended up in his band. Plus, when Dizzy Gillespie came out here earlier and played the Pasadena Civic Auditorium it was quite a band. And I think Roy knew that our big band could be just as bad as those cats from Diz's band.

We started rehearsing at the Chicken Shack on Vernon and Avalon. Since I was going to school, rehearsals were in late afternoon. Sometimes we would showcase the band in the afternoons and the place would be packed. We played Billy Berg's in Hollywood, which was nice. But other times we'd only make three dollars – and if we made ten dollars we were doing great. After the tour and accident I left in early 1950 to go out with Charles Brown. We played the Black and Tan nightclub in San Diego where Paul Sparks and I got busted. While I was gone either Hadley Caliman or Boogie Daniels took my chair. It was like platooning on a baseball team – three people for one position.

We recorded for Savoy in 1949 with me and Joe Howard. But the Knockout session featured Hadley Caliman, since I was out with Charles Brown. Our arranger Joe Howard didn't have any formal training. It all came from within. Robert Ross, our other arranger, got his training from the army bands. He had more experience than Joe, but they were both bad. Later when Robert Ross and I were incarcerated at Terminal Island, he showed me a lot of pointers about writing.

Being with Roy Porter's 17 Beboppers gave me my first
big-band experience, my first recording experience and my
first tour. Plus, it was more like a family. When we left LA on
our tour we were ready to tear New York up. We had the
attitude that Diz's band wasn't that bad because we had a
conga player too, Alvy Kidd, who could also play drums
when Roy didn't. We also had a guitar player named Benny
White who gave the rhythm section the full sound, so we
were some cocky young dudes.

We left LA for some dates that Paul Sparks's brother Jerry
had set up for us. We played Phoenix, Arizona, the first
night and the band cooked. We picked up a trombone player
by the name of Herman Relf in Phoenix on our way to El
Paso, Texas. Jerry Sparks had this big black 1941 Buick
Century. I even remember the licence number, CA 8E237.
Clyde "Thin Man" Tillis had this old 1938 Cadillac and Roy,
Art, Clyde Dunn, Cisco and the driver were in a 1941 brown
or tan Buick. When we got to Deming, New Mexico, the
Buick had an accident and Roy, Clyde and Art got hurt.
Cisco and the driver didn't get a scratch. That meant that the
leader, first trumpet player and baritone sax man were out
for good, because they were all taken to the hospital at
Deming.

We went on and tried to play the gig at El Paso. That night
at the concert Leroy "Sweetpea" Robinson cried all through
the performance because the band didn't sound the same.
He was such a soulful cat. He was playing so pretty and sad
that he had everyone in the band crying along with him. All
his tears came out through his horn – Sweetpea.

We made it to Lawton, Oklahoma, where we stayed at the
USO. Fort Sill Army Base is located there. Then we started
playing gigs for the door so we could get food and gas to get
us back to Deming to pick up the guys at the hospital.

The bass player we got for this tour was called Tony Cold
Cuts, because he could always take the small change we
made and go to the store and come back with cold cuts,
salami, cheese and crackers. He helped us make it. But
actually Wiggie Wiginton's knowledge pulled us through.
Wiggie and Robert Ross were older and their experience

proved invaluable. Whenever we would be about to run out of gas we would put on a concert just for the door admission. This was one of Wiggie's survival ideas. We got through Lawton after about a week. Then we got to Hobbs, New Mexico, where we picked up Roy, Art and Clyde from the hospital. When we had everybody back together we headed out of there and cold cutted it on back to Los Angeles.

That was our first experience on how life can be out on the road. But all in all it was a good experience. When we got back I went back to Phoenix on another gig, but joined Lionel Hampton when he came through there. The first gig we played was at El Paso. When we passed the spot where the accident had taken place I told all of the guys on the bus all about it.

I didn't stay on with Hamp at that time, but went with him later in 1953, when he made his first European tour. Art Farmer and I joined then. Quincy Jones was in that band, along with Benny Bailey, Buster Cooper, Tony Ortega, Jimmy Cleveland, Morris Lane and both Wes and Monk Montgomery. But the real irony of this is that later in 1955 when I was up in Alaska Lionel Hampton had an accident at that very spot where the Roy Porter Big Band had their mishap. Billy Brooks, the trumpet player, was hurt and the bus driver was killed from a heart attack. It was very ironic, almost like a Bermuda Triangle situation.

JOE SPARKS

My brother Paul was the vocalist with the Roy Porter Big Band but I didn't come in contact with Roy directly until one evening when I found that there was some electrical equipment missing from my shop. Paul had taken some lights and cords to Roy's rehearsal. He'd left a note that they were rehearsing at Nardoni Bates's record store at 41st and Central.

I got to the rehearsal and Roy said, "Man, I'm sure glad you showed up, because these lights are sure funky." It wasn't that the lights were bad, they just didn't have the clips on them. These guys were about to electrocute themselves.

My older brother, Jerry, was in the process of booking some one-nighters for the band down through Arizona, New Mexico, Oklahoma, on up to Chicago, but he didn't really have the experience for this endeavor. So, since I'd had some road experience I agreed to go along as far as Oklahoma.

We left Los Angeles in four cars and a truck for the instruments, which I drove. We played one night in Phoenix at the Elks Auditorium. The promoters tried to pull a fast one on us by telling us that not many tickets had been sold. But they outsmarted themselves when they couldn't outdrink me. So, we left Phoenix in good financial shape. Our gig for the following night was at El Paso, Texas. But when we got to the outskirts of Deming, New Mexico, the accident occurred. To this day I feel responsible for it because I was leading the caravan. Roy had to be in El Paso at a certain time that night to make a radio broadcast for the dance. I'd told the drivers to try to keep up with me because of the broadcast, but I let the car that Roy, Art Farmer, Clyde Dunn and Cisco were in pass me. This particular stretch of highway had long, deep dips in it and soft shoulders. After Roy's car passed me I was way behind them, back with the rest of the cars, when I looked up and all I could see was a cloud of dust ahead. When we got to the scene, Roy was laying over on one side of the highway, Clyde was thrown to the other side, and Art Farmer was laying on one of the doors. Cisco and the driver didn't have a scratch. The car was doing 80 miles an hour and had a blow out and turned over three times. These people were very lucky to be alive. The scene of the accident was like a scene in a war zone. When the Highway Patrol got there they were very understanding. After Roy, Art and Clyde were taken to the hospital, the Highway Patrol radioed El Paso and explained the situation to some other troopers, who met us at the El Paso city limits and red-lighted the band into the city. It turned out that Roy was the most seriously injured, with four broken ribs, while Clyde Dunn and Art Farmer each suffered concussion.

After the dance in El Paso we went to Hobbs, New Mexico, as a rest stop. I had relatives there and they put up the band for a few days. While there we booked a dance for the weekend, when we'd be back from our engagement in Lawton, Oklahoma. In the meantime I went back to Los Angeles to pick up another car. Along the way I checked in on Roy, Art and Clyde in Deming. The band played a few dates in Lawton, but the going got tough without Roy, Art and Clyde on the baritone sax. We were in Lawton about a week and then went back to Hobbs for the weekend dance. Roy, Art and Clyde were picked up from the hospital in Deming, but of course they were in no shape to play. We left Hobbs and came back to Los Angeles, where Roy went into the VA hospital for a week. It was a hell of an experience being out on the road with that big band.

ROGER HAMILTON SPOTTS

I was born and raised in Cincinnati, Ohio. There were a lot of good musicians then in that city – Frank Foster, Billy Brooks, Curtis Peagler and others. Frank had a band that I was in, but he always took all the sax solos himself. So I started writing some of my own arrangements and gave myself some solos. After graduating from Central State University, I was drafted and was sent overseas during the Korean conflict. While I was on leave in 1952 I saw Roy Porter at Bop City in San Francisco. When I got out I taught school for a while at Fairfield High in Alabama, then in 1955 I came to Los Angeles, but not to play music. I came because I wanted to see what Los Angeles was like.

By this time I was playing piano as well as tenor and I started gigging with many people. Some of the name musicians in LA were Gerald Wilson, Teddy Edwards, Roy, Hampton Hawes, Sonny Criss and Dexter Gordon. There were others who weren't yet recorded, who were also quite talented, like Carl Perkins, Dupree Bolton, Art Farmer,

Frank Morgan, Walter Benton, Lester Robertson and Horace Tapscott.

But when I used to play with Jesse Price he'd always talk so bad to me. I'd respect his seniority and keep silent until one night when he said, "You little jive-ass motherfucker, shut up. You're not even dry behind your ears yet."

I replied, "I'm dry behind my ass, so kiss my ass."

He said, "Oh. You're alright." We got along fine from then on. Jesse was known for his bad mouth, but everyone still loved him.

The first gig I worked with Roy was with Theodore Rudolph and his Four Bits of Rhythm band. We played dance and lounge-type of music. One night at the Windemer Hotel in Santa Monica we were playing *Night Train* with the piano triplet back-beat. Roy started something on his sock cymbal, and with his left hand and the bass drum he gave it a double-time feeling, but he still kept the back-beat going. I'd never heard this before. Roy later told me that it was something he'd been wanting to try. Now you hear it on many rock records. I admire Roy because, though he was primarily a jazz drummer, he was able to adjust to most any musical situation. After that we became close associates.

Discography

Abbreviations

arr	arranger
g	guitar
as	alto saxophone
p	piano
b	double bass
perc	percussion
bar	baritone saxophone
syn	synthesizer
bs	bass saxophone
t	trumpet
d	drums
tb	trombone
ep	electric piano
ts	tenor saxophone
f	flute
v	vocal
flh	flugelhorn
vib	vibraphone

1945   4 September   Hollywood

Howard McGhee

Howard McGhee (t); Teddy Edwards, James King (ts); Vernon Biddle (p); Bob Kesterson (b); Roy Porter (d)

Van 200	Intersection	Philo 117
Van 201	Lifestream	Philo 116
Van 202	Mop Mop	Philo 118
Van 203	Stardust	Philo 115

1945   September Hollywood

Howard McGhee Big Band

As above, with Snooky Young, Karl George (t); Vic Dickenson, Gene Roland (tb); Robert Isabell, Gene Porter (as, bar)

M136A-3	Cool Fantasy, pt.1	Modern Music LP20-618
M136B-2	Cool Fantasy, pt.2	–
M137	McGhee Special	Modern Music 136

1945   Los Angeles

Howard McGhee

Howard McGhee (t); Teddy Edwards (ts); Vernon Biddle (p); Bob Kesterson (b); Roy Porter (d)

	McGhee Special	Modern Music
	Mad Hype	
	11.45 Swing	
	Playboy Blues	
	Around the Clock	
	Gee I'm Lonesome	
	Call it the Blues	
	McGhee Jumps	
	Cool Fantasy	

1946   Hollywood

Howard McGhee

Howard McGhee (t); Teddy Edwards (ts); Vernon Biddle (p); Bob Kesterson (b); Roy Porter (d)

BN22	Mad Hype	Modern Music LP20-618
BN23	Rummage Bounce	Modern Music 120
	(11.45 Swing)	

1946   Hollywood

Howard McGhee

Howard McGhee (t); Teddy Edwards, James King (ts);Vernon Biddle (p); Bob Kesterson (b); Roy Porter (d);

Pearl Traylor, Estelle Edson, Clarence Williams (v)

Playboy Blues (PT, v)	Modern Music 120
Around the Clock, pt.1 (PT, v)	Modern Music 124
Around the Clock, pt.2	–
Gee I'm Lonesome (PT, v)	Modern Music 125
Call it the Blues (EE, v)	–
The Jive I Like (PT, v)	Modern Music 127
I'm Drunk (CW, v)	–

1946   Los Angeles

Estelle Edson

Estelle Edson (v), with Karl George (t); Jewell Grant (as); Lucky Thompson (ts); possibly L. Beck (bar); Wilbert Baranco (p); Charlie Norris (g); Oscar Pettiford (b); Roy Porter (d)

BW163	Be-baba-le-ba	Black & White 760
BW164	Rhythm in a Riff	–
BW165	I Changed the Lock on the Door	Black & White 761
BW166	Don't Drive this Jive Away	–

1946   28 March   Hollywood

Charlie Parker

Miles Davis (t); Charlie Parker (as); Lucky Thompson (ts); Dodo Marmarosa (p); Arvin Garrison (g); Vic McMillan (b); Roy Porter (d)

D1010-1	Moose the Mooche (AG out)	Dial LP201
D1010-2	Moose the Mooche (AG out)	Dial 1003
D1010-3	Moose the Mooche (AG out)	Spotlite SPJ105
D1011-1	Yardbird Suite	Dial LP201
D1011-2	Yardbird Suite	unissued
D1011-3	Yardbird Suite	unissued
D1011-4	Yardbird Suite	Dial 1003
D1012-1	Ornithology	Dial LP208
D1012-2	Ornithology	unissued
D1012-3	Ornithology (Bird Lore)	Dial 1006
D1012-4	Ornithology	Dial 1002
D1013-1	Famous Alto Break	Dial LP905
D1013-2	Night in Tunisia	unissued
D1013-3	Night in Tunisia	unissued

| D1013-4 | Night in Tunisia | Dial LP201 |
| D1013-5 | Night in Tunisia | Dial 1002 |

1946   Spring   Hollywood
Howard McGhee

*Howard McGhee (t); James King (ts, v); Teddy Edwards (ts);
Jimmy Bunn (p); Bob Kesterson (b); Roy Porter (d)*

KF1-23333	Sweet Potato	Melodisc M-1001
KF1-23337	Hoggin'	Melodisc M-1002
KF1-23345	Blues à la King (JK, v)	–
KF1-26610	Night Mist	Melodisc M-1001

1946   29 July   Hollywood
Charlie Parker

*Howard McGhee (t); Charlie Parker (as); Jimmy Bunn (p);
Bob Kesterson (b); Roy Porter (d)*

D1021-A	Max Making Wax	Dial LP201
D1022-A	Lover Man	Dial 1007
D1023-A	The Gypsy	Dial 1043

1946   29 July   Hollywood
Howard McGhee

As above

D1024-A	Bebop	Dial 1007
D1025-B	Trumpet at Tempo (CP out)	Dial 1005
D1026-C	Thermodynamics (CP out)	Dial 1020

1946   Summer   San Francisco
Ernie Lewis

*Ernie Royal (t); possibly Sonny Criss (as); Wardell Gray (ts);
Ernie Lewis (p); Vernon Alley (b); possibly Roy Porter (d)*

| Vernon Alley's Blues | Pacific Jazz 610 |
| Hit That Jive Jack | – |

1946   18 October   Hollywood

Howard McGhee

Howard McGhee (t); Teddy Edwards (ts); Dodo Marmarosa (p); Arvin Garrison (g); Bob Kesterson (b); Roy Porter (d)

D1041-4	High Wind in Hollywood	Dial 1012
D1041-5	Dialated Pupils	Dial 1011
D1042-4	Midnite at Minton's	–
D1043-1	Up in Dodo's Room	Dial 1010
D1043-2	Up in Dodo's Room	–
D1044-2	High Wind in Hollywood (52nd Street Theme)	–

1947   9 March   Hi-de-Ho Club, Los Angeles

Howard McGhee

Howard McGhee (t); Charlie Parker (as); Hampton Hawes (p); Addison Farmer (b); Roy Porter (d)

Dee Dee's Dance, pt.1	Spotlite SPJ107
Dee Dee's Dance, pt.2	–

1947   6 July   Elk's Auditorium, Los Angeles

Hollywood Jazz Concert

Howard McGhee (t); Trummy Young (tb); Sonny Criss (as); Dexter Gordon, Wardell Gray (ts); Hampton Hawes (p); Barney Kessel (g); Red Callender (b); Roy Porter (d)

bop36	Bopland I	Savoy 962
bop37	Bopland II	–
bop38	Bopland III	Savoy 963
bop39	Bopland IV	–
bop40	Bopland V	Savoy 964
bop41	Bopland VI	–
bop42	Jeronimo I	Bop 111
bop43	Jeronimo II	–
bop44	Jeronimo III	Bop 112
bop45	Jeronimo IV	–
bop46	Jeronimo V	Bop 113
bop47	Jeronimo VI	–
bop48	Jeronimo VII	Bop 114

| bop49 | Jeronimo VIII | – |

Wardell Gray out

bop54	Bop After Hours I	Bop 115
bop55	Bop After Hours II	–
bop56	Bop After Hours III	Bop 116
bop57	Bop After Hours IV	–
bop58	Bop After Hours V	Bop 117
bop59	Bop After Hours VI	–

NB: "Bopland" later issued as "Byas-a-Drink"; "Jeronimo" later issued as "Cherrykoke" and "Cherokee"
bop36-49 were re-released under the names of Gordon and Gray on *The Hunt* (Savoy SJL222) and bop 54-9 under Gordon's name on *Long Tall Dexter* (Savoy SJL2211).

1947   4 December   Los Angeles

Teddy Edwards

Teddy Edwards (ts); Jimmie Rowles (p); Red Callender (b); Roy Porter (d)

| D1145AA | Blues in Teddy's Flat | Dial 1033 |

1947   4 December   Los Angeles

Dexter Gordon

Dexter Gordon (ts); Jimmie Rowles (p); Red Callender (b); Roy Porter (d)

D1141-C	Ghost of a Chance	Spotlite SPJ133
D1141-D	Ghost of a Chance	Dial LP204
D1141-E	Ghost of a Chance	Dial 1018
D1142-A	Sweet and Lovely	Dial LP204
D1142-D	Sweet and Lovely	Dial 1042

Roy suggests that *Talk of the Town* was also recorded on this date.

Add Teddy Edwards (ts)

D1143-C	The Duel, pt.1 (Hornin' In)	Dial LP204
D1143-DD	The Duel, pt.1	Dial 1028
D1144-C	The Duel, pt.2 (Hornin' In)	Dial LP204
D1144-DF	The Duel, pt.2	Dial 1028

1947   cMarch   Los Angeles

Howard McGhee

Howard McGhee (t); Sonny Criss (as); Teddy Edwards (ts); Hampton Hawes (p); Addison Farmer (b); Roy Porter (d)

	Ornithology	Jazz Showcase Records 5005
	Body and Soul	–
	The Man I Love	–

1947   cJune   Los Angeles

Joe Lutcher

Parr Jones (t); Joe Lutcher (as, v); Bill Ellis (ts); Harold Morrow (p); Bill Cooper (b); Dick Hart (d); Roy Porter (bongo)

MM1005	Rock-ola	Modern Music 20-661
MM1006	Pasadena Rhumboogie	–
MM1031	Goin' to the Mardi Gras	–
	Blues for Sale	Specialty 304

1947   July   Los Angeles

Teddy Edwards

Benny Bailey (t); Teddy Edwards (ts); Duke Brooks (p); Addison Farmer (b); Roy Porter (d)

MR-5	Bird Legs	Rex Records 25056
MR-6	Out of Nowhere	–
MR-7	Roy's Boy	Rex Records 25057
MR-8	Steady with Teddy	–
	Rexology	Rex Records 25058
	Three Bass Hit	–
	R. B.'s Wig	Rex Records 25059
	Body and Soul	–

1947/8   Los Angeles

Teddy Edwards

Herbie Harper (tb); Teddy Edwards (ts); Hampton Hawes (p); Iggy Shevack (b); Roy Porter (d)

Teddy's Tune	Rex 26025
Wonderful Work	–
Fairy Dance	Rex 26026
It's the Talk of the Town	–

1949   29 January   Hollywood

Roy Porter Big Band

*Art Farmer, Bob Ross, Eddie Preston, James Metlock (t);
Jimmy Knepper, Danny Horton, William Wiginton (tb);
Leroy Robinson, Eric Dolphy (as); Joe Howard, Clifford
Solomon (ts); Clyde Dunn (bs); Joe Harrison (p); Ben White
(g); Roger Alderson (b); Roy Porter (d); Alvy Kidd (conga);
Paul Sparks (v)*

SLA1100	Pete's Beat	Savoy MG9026
SLA1101	Sippin' with Cisco, pt.1	Savoy SJL2215
SLA1102	Sippin' with Cisco, pt.2	–
SLA1103	This is You (PS, v)	–
SLA1104	Gassin' the Wig	Savoy 944

1949   18 February   Los Angeles

Dee Williams

*John Anderson (t); Gene Montgomery (ts); Richard Brom
(bs); Devonia Williams (p); Charles Norris (g); Morris
Edwards (b); Roy Porter (d)*

SLA	Central Avenue Hop	
SLA505-3	Dee's Boogi	Savoy 684
SLA506-1	Bongo Blues	–
SLA508-1	Midnite Creep	Savoy 716
SLA509-1	Double Trouble Hop	–
SLA510	L.A. Shuffle	
SLA511	Blow, Gene, Blow	

NB: Savoy 716 issued under the name California Playboys

1949   23 February   Los Angeles

Roy Porter Big Band

Personnel as for session of 29 January 1949

SLA512	Phantom Moon	Savoy SJL2215
SLA513	Howard's Idea	–
SLA514	Love is Laughing at Me (PS, v)	–
SLA515-4	Little Wig	Savoy 994

1948/9   Los Angeles

Roy Porter Big Band

Personnel as above, except for Addison Farmer (b)

Minor Mode	unissued
This is You	–
Love is Laughing at Me	–
A Sunday Kind of Love	–

1949   Los Angeles

Roy Porter Big Band

| Don't Blame Me | Rex Hollywood 28002 |

1950   Spring   Los Angeles

Roy Porter Big Band

*Art Farmer, Reuben McFall, Robert Ross, Kenny Bright (t);
William Wiginton, Jimmy Knepper, Danny Horton (tb); Eric
Dolphy, Joe Maini (as); Joe Howard, Hadley Caliman (ts);
Toy Ortega (bar); Russ Freeman (p); Harold Grant (g, v);
Addison Farmer (b); Roy Porter (d); Mike Pacheco (conga,
bongo, perc)*

	Hunter's Hunters	Knockout Records
	Blues à la Carte	
K107	Moods at Dusk	
K108	Sampson's Creep	

1950   9 August   Los Angeles

Mighty Man Maxwell

*Mighty Man Maxwell (v); Paul Madison (ts); Charles Waller
(bs); Lester Myart (p); Edgar Rice (g); Eddie Williams (b);
Roy Porter (d)*

| D328 | I Feel Like Shouting | Discovery 524 |
| D329 | Goodnight Irene | – |

1950   9 August   Los Angeles

Eddie Williams

Lester Myart (p, v); Edgar Rice (g); Eddie Williams (b); Roy Porter (bongo)

| D330 | Mandering | Discovery 526 |
| D331 | Blues for Cuba | – |

1955   1 September   Hollywood

Tony Allen

Tony Allen (v); Hubert Myers (ts); Zebedee Kindred (p); Williams Pyks (g); Duke Harris (b); Roy Porter (d)

	Night Owl	Specialty 560
	I	–
	Check Yourself Baby	Specialty 570
	Especially	–

1957   Hollywood

Roy Porter

Sonny Criss (as); Roy Porter (o, p, v); Buddy Woodson (b); Al Bartee (d)

	Wow	Debonair
	Got a Funny Feelin'	
	Minor Moods	
	Love You	

1957   2 February   Los Angeles

Earl Bostic

John Anderson, Ronnie Lewis (t); Earl Bostic, Jewell Grant (as); William Green, Teddy Edwards (ts); Charlie Lawrence (p); Adolphus Alsbrook (b); Roy Porter (d); Larry Bunker (vib); Billy Jones (v)

K9934-1	How Deep is the Ocean	King LP558
K9935-4	Avalon	–
K9936-2	Too Fine for Crying (BJ, v)	–
K9937	Away	King LP547

1957   28 February   Los Angeles

Earl Bostic

As above, plus Irving Ashby (g); Lou Singer (vib) replaces Bunker; -1 v chorus

K9947-2	Temptation	King LP 547
K9948-2	Exercise	–
K9949-2	She's Funny That Way	–
K9950-1	September Song -1	–

c1957   Los Angeles

Little Richard

Other personnel unknown

Tutti Frutti
Long Tall Sally

1959   Los Angeles

Roy Porter

Jimmy Allen (ts); Roy Porter (p, d); Herman Mitchell, Harold Grant (g); Clarence Daniels (b)

Roy's Blues (RP, p)   Pico 521
Home Cookin'   –

c1959   Los Angeles

Roy Porter

Same personnel as above

Good Cookin   Amazon Records
Summer Night
You Do This to Me
Juicy

1961   Los Angeles

The Titans

Joe Sample (p); Sonny Kenner (g); Bob West (b); Roy Porter (d); Larry Green, Curtis McNear (v)

Lonesome Mood	World Pacific
Just the One	
Blues for Dee	
Romayne	
April in Paris	

1962   Los Angeles

Jennell Hawkins

Bob Tate (as); Jimmy Allen (ts, f); Jennell Hawkins (o, v); Sonny Kenner (g); Roy Porter (d)

Can I	Amazon AM1001
Moments to Remember	–
Ol' Man River	–
Where or When	–
Every Day	–
Blue Moon	–
How Does it Feel	–
In the Groove	–

1964   Hollywood

Joe Liggins

Jake Porter (t); Bill Green, Willie Jackson (as); Jackie Kelso (ts); Floyd Turnham (bar); Joe Liggins (p); Harold Grant (g); Red Callender (b); Roy Porter (d)

Tanya	Mercury MG20731
Honeydripper, pt.1	–
Honeydripper, pt.2	–
If You Really Love Me	–
I've Got a Right to Cry	–
Pink Champagne	–
Barnyard Imitation	–

Frankie Lee	–
Friday Night Twist Party	–
Black Coffee Blues	–
Wee Hours	–
Sharing My Days	–

1971   Los Angeles

Roy Porter

Hense Powell, James Smith (t, flh); Lester Robertson (tb); Jack H. Fulks (ts, f); Sone Campbell (ts); Tollie Moore, Jr (p); Bob Davis (o); Jimmy Holloway, Leslie Hargrove (g); Charlie Jones (b); Roy Porter (d); Oscar Dye (conga); Arne Frager, Jamie Wilson (syn)

Jessica	Chelan CHPS2501
Funky Twitch	–
Hip City	–
Hence Forth	–
Drums for Daryl	–
Wow	–
Ooh-la-la	–

1975   March   Los Angeles

Roy Porter

Hense Powell (t, arr); Hugh Bell (t); Wallace Huff (tb); Jack Fulks (ts, f); Prince Harrison, Charlemagne Payne, Jimmy Allen (ts); Clyde Dunn (bar); Tollie Moore (ep); Randy Pigge Herman Mitchell, Harold Grant (g); Charlie Jones, Clarence Daniels (b); Arne Frager (b, syn); Roy Porter (d, perc, v); Roy Thompson, Demond Gates (d); Frank Mastrapa (conga)

Party Time	Bel-Ad 1006
Love You	–
Panama	–
Jessica	–
Wavering	–
Funny Feelin'	–
Out on the Town Tonight	–
Givin' Me the Blues	–

1978   Los Angeles

Sonny Til and the Orioles

Personnel unknown

    Back to the Chapel   Dobre Records 1026

Bibliography

Gardner, Mark: "Jazz Scene," *Melody Maker* (London, 19 December 1970)

----: "Musicians Talking," *Jazz & Blues* (London, July, August & September 1971)

Gibson, Gertrude: "A Roy Porter Happening," *Los Angeles Sentinel* (21 January 1971)

Kirkwood, Johnny: "My Night Out," *This is L.A.* (Los Angeles, 14 January 1971)

Patterson, Owen: "Artistry of Dodo Marmarosa," *Jazz & Blues* (London, April 1972)

Shields, Jim: "The Roy Porter Story," *Scoop* (Los Angeles, 7 December 1972)

Scott, Dahle: "Who's Who," *Scoop* (Los Angeles, 8 January 1976)

Service, Brenda: "Roy Porter," *Cause* (Los Angeles, January & February 1976)

Simosko, Vladimir and Tepperman, Barry: *Eric Dolphy: a Musical Biography and Discography* (New York, Da Capo, 1979)

Keller, David: "Eric Dolphy: the Los Angeles Years," *Jazz Times* (Silver Spring, MD, November 1981)

Driggs, Frank and Lewine, Harris: *Black Beauty, White Heat: a Pictorial History of Classic Jazz, 1920–1950* (New York, Morrow, 1982)

Priestley, Brian: *Mingus: a Critical Biography* (London, 1982)

Keller, David: "Black California," *Coda* (Toronto, no. 188, 1983)

----: "An Interview with Roy Porter," *Jazz Heritage* (Los Angeles, September & October 1983)

Green, John: "The Porter Principal," *Bebop & Beyond* (Los Angeles, November & December 1984)

Marmorstein, Gary: "Playing it Hot: the Coming of Age of L.A.'s Jazz Scene," *California Living/Los Angeles Herald* (18 November 1984)

Gitler, Ira: *From Swing to Bop* (New York, 1985)

Mansfield, Horace and Mack, Gerald: "Roy Porter," *Bebop & Beyond* (Los Angeles, July & August 1985)

Poindexter, Pony: *The Pony Express: Memoirs of a Jazz Musician* (Frankfurt, J.A.S., 1985)

Klett, Shirley: "Roy Porter," *Cadence* (Redwood, NY, September & October 1986)

Snowden, Don: "Central Avenue," *L.A. Style* (November 1987)

Index